CHARMING SMALL

TUSCANY

&

UMBRIA

CHARMING SMALL HOTEL GUIDES

TUSCANY &
UMBRIA

Including Florence and Siena

EDITED BY

Fiona Duncan & Leonie Glass

Interlink Books
An imprint of Interlink Publishing Group, Inc.
New York • Northampton

4th expanded & redesigned edition

First American edition published in 2003 by
Interlink Books
An imprint of Interlink Publishing Group, Inc.
46 Crosby Street, Northampton, Massachusetts 01060
www.interlinkbooks.com

This series is conceived, designed and produced by
Duncan Petersen Publishing Ltd.,
31 Ceylon Road, London W14 OPY

Editorial Director Andrew Duncan
Editors Fiona Duncan & Leonie Glass
Contributing Editor Nicola Swallow
Production Editor Nicola Davies
Art Editor Don Macpherson

Library of Congress Cataloging-in-Publication Data available
ISBN 1-56656-502-2

Printed and bound in Italy

To request our complete 48-page full-color catalog, please call us toll
free at 1-800-238-LINK, visit our website at www.interlinkbooks.com,
or send us an e-mail: info@interlinkbooks.com

CONTENTS

INTRODUCTION

Welcome to this new edition of the first regional guide in the now well-established Charming Small Hotel Guides series. In covering an area, rather than a whole country, we did so in depth, using only a few of the places featured in our all-Italy guide - those entries we could not ignore. The majority of the places featured in this guide do not appear in our all-Italy guide.

Charming and small

There really are relatively few genuine charming small hotels. Unlike other guides, we are particularly fussy about size. In Italy, even family-run hotels seem to grow inevitably and the ten-room hotel is a rarity, but most of our recommendations have fewer than 30 rooms. If a hotel has more than that, it needs to have the feel of a much smaller place to be in this guide.

We attach more importance to size than other guides because we think that unless a hotel is small, it cannot give a genuinely personal welcome, or make you feel like an individual, rather than just a guest. For what we mean by a personal welcome, see below.

Unlike other gudes, we often rule out places that have great qualitites, but are nonetheless no more nor less than – hotels. Our hotels are all special in some way.

We think that we have a much clearer idea than other guides of what is special and what is not; and we think we apply these criteria more consistently than other guides because we are a small and personally managed company rather than a bureaucracy. We have a small team of like-minded inspectors, chosen by the editor and thoroughly rehearsed in recognizing what we want. While we very much appreciate reader' reports – see page 182 – they are not our main source of information.

Last but by no means least, we're independent – there's no payment for inclusion.

Tuscany and Umbria for the traveller

It is not difficult to recognize why we chose Tuscany and Umbria as the first regional guide for the series. The region is favoured, par excellence, both with natural and man-made landscapes of incomparable beauty and variety, and its artistic heritage is unequalled in the world. From the Tuscan Coast with its white beaches and pine-shaded coasts to Chianti's rolling hills teeming with cypresses, olives and vines to Umbria, Italy's green heart, visitors will find any form of nature to suit their taste. Travellers through the Garfagnana, in the north-western corner of Tuscany, often think that they have accidentally strayed into some dramatic part of the Alps; while in the still under-explored Maremma, to the south-west, they find cowboys on horse-back tending their herds.

Dotted across the whole region are, of course, many of Italy's most famous citta d'arte (art cities), whose names everone knows: Florence, Siena, Volterra, San Gimignano, Perugia, Assisi and

So what exactly do we look for?

- *A peaceful, attractive setting in an interesting and picturesque position.*

- *A building that is either handsome or interesting or historic, or at least with a distinct character.*

- *Bedrooms that are well proportioned with as much character as the public rooms below.*

- *Ideally, we look for adequate space, but on a human scale: we don't go for places that rely on grandeur, or that have pretensions that could intimidate.*

- *Decorations must be harmonious and in good taste, and the furnishings and facilities comfortable and well maintained. We like to see interesting antique furniture that is there because it can be used, not simply revered.*

- *The proprietors and staff need to be dedicated and thoughtful, offering a personal welcome, without being intrusive. The guest needs to feel like an individual.*

Gubbio. But these are only the diamonds in the tiara (and perhaps suffering in recent years from the depredations of mass tourism – they are best seen out of high season unless your idea of a holiday is to stand in long queues for a three-minute ogle of David).

Less well-known gems abound throughout the two regions: Montefalco, known as Umbria's balcony for its remarkable outlook; Trevi, with its dramatic mountain-side location; Pienza, a delightful and unique remainder of Renaissance town planning; and San Piero a Sieve, in the Mugello, whose ugly outskirts belie its medieval heart.

Much of the delight of travelling this region lies in ignoring the standard tourist trails and just following the road. Do this, and you will always be sure of arriving at some memorable destination which, may well not yet be 'discovered' – by the tourists, or the guide books.

Entries, long and short

The full-page entries with colour photographs are our warmest recommendations BUT the short (three-a-page) entries on pages 145-181 are all charming small hotels, and by no means second class. Think of them as silver- or bronze-medallists (a world full of gold medallists would be intolerably boring). They have all, like the long entries, been inspected, and selected for inclusion in the guide because they satisfy our criteria.

Hotels, villas, locande, agriturismo,

The range of accommodation on offer in Tuscany and Umbria should be enough to satisfy all tastes and most pockets, with a variety of names almost as numerous as those describing types of pasta. 'Hotel' is common enough, but so is its Italian equivalent 'albergo'. 'Villa' can apply either to a town or country hotel and is used by proprietors with some latitude: occasionally one wonders why a nondescript town house or farmhouse should be called a villa while a more elegant building restricts itself to albergo. 'Palazzo' and 'pensione' generally refer to urban accommodation while 'agriturismo' means farmhouse bed-and-breakfast, or indeed, self-catering apartments. 'Residence', 'relais', 'locanda', 'castello' and 'fattoria' are also found.

The variety that one finds under these various names is extraordinary, from world-ranking luxury hotels to relatively simple guest-houses.

Bedrooms and bathrooms

Most of the hotels in this guide are found in old buildings, whether they be farmhouses, medieval castles or towers, Renaissance villas and palazzi, former monasteries or just a solid edifice from the 19thC. This guarantees individuality, but it also means that, in the same hotel, the standards of rooms can vary greatly, as, occasionally, do prices. When writing to the hotel, state your requirements - not every monk's cell in a former monastery is blessed with a view. And neither, originally, would it have had a bath room en suite. For the most part, these have been added without undue intrusiveness, but they tend not to be spacious, at least by American standards.

Style varies, but Italians are a meticulously clean people and no bedrooms and bathrooms should be less than acceptable.

Food

Strangely enough, the one place in Italy where a cup of coffee can be disappointing is in a hotel. The pre-prepared beverage lacks the intense flavour of a freshly-made espresso or steaming cappuccino, so if you are fussy about your first cup of the day, ask for one of these. Bed-and-breakfasts tend to serve 'moka' coffee, made in the characteristic aluminium pot found in all Italian households. In hotels, self-service buffet breakfasts are common, with everything available from cereals to salami, and are ideal for travellers who may not eat properly again until the evening. Most Italians start the day with a cappuccino and a brioche, and in some establishments this may be all you are offered.

Half board is rarely obligatory and often not available, even if the hotel has a restaurant attached, as most visitors like to sample the wide variety of restaurants in an area.

Your host and hostess

Nearly every place we visited claimed to speak English, though sometimes it was not clear what level of fluency was involved. Do not worry: the more professional hotels all have staff with some degree of proficiency and for the rest, Italians are irrepressible communicators across any number of linguistic and cultural barriers. If you can offer a few phrases of Italian, it will usually work wonders.

Travel facts

The tourist information offices for each province are listed with the relevant maps on pages 14-32. Most cities and a few popular towns also have their own tourist offices offering information on local travel, museums, galleries and fiestas.

Flights

The principal airports for Tuscany are at Pisa and Florence, and car hire is available at both. Pisa airport is connected directly to Florence by an hourly train service. Florence airport has a less satisfactory bus connection to the centre. If you are staying in town, try to share a taxi.

Umbria has no major airport of its own, but there is a small one near Perugia. You can fly there from Pisa or Florence airports, or from Rome or Rimini.

Pets

Even if the fact box following the description says 'pets accepted', please notify when booking that you want to take a pet. No hotelier wants a pack of hounds racing around the foyer, and many only allow small dogs, kept exclusively to the guest's own room.

Electricity

The norm is 220-volt-50-cycles. U.S. visitors will need electrical converters (or dual voltage appliances). Most bathrooms do not supply hair-driers. Two plug sizes operate in Italy, so be sure to bring an adaptor.

Smoking

Nobody seems to know what the law is, or how it should be interpreted, and at the time of writing a free-for-all reigns with very few exceptions. Some hotels have a non-smoking area; it may be the case that by the time this guide is published smoking will be banned in public places, although it would be naive to expect this rule to be rigorously observed.

How to find an entry

In the first part of the guide are the long entries, first in Tuscany, then in Umbria.

Within these sections, the hotels are listed alphabetically, 1 by province; 2 by town or local government district (comune); and 3

by the name of the hotel. The short entries at the back of the
guide are organized in a similar way.
There are three easy ways to find a hotel:

* Use the maps on pages 14-32. Each number on a map refers to
the page on which the hotel is featured.

* If you know the area you want to visit, browse through that sec-
tion until you find a place that meets your requirements.

* Use the indexes at the back of the book. They list entries both
by hotel name (page 192) and by location (page 199).

How to read an entry
At the top of each page is the relevant region (Tuscany or Umbria);
below that is the province; then follows the type of hotel and its
town or district and, finally, the name of the hotel itself.
   In the case of Florence, which is both the largest city and an
important province, we use the English name for the town and
the Italian name, Firenze, for the province.
The description then follows.

Fact boxes
Following the description are facts and figures that should help
you to decide if the hotel is in your price range and has the facilities you want.
   First comes the the address. 'Loc.' stands for locality (localitá
in Italian) and indicates the area near a town where the hotel is
situated. The name of the town is generally the name of the
comune (the local administrative unit) and these can cover quite
a large area, especially in rural parts. You should be armed with a
map. We recommend the Atlante Stradale d'Italia - Centro, published by the Touring Club Italiano.
   The address concludes with the postal code and the name of
the province (abbreviated in Italian to a two-letter code).

Tel and fax
The number in brackets is the area code within Italy. If you are
calling from abroad, you must include the zero after the international code for Italy (39).

Location
The location and setting of the hotel are briefly described; car
parking facilities follow. In Florence, few hotels have their own
car parking, and depend on arrangements with nearby garages.
The prices are set by the garages and not by the hotels, so please
check first.

Prices
The range of prices is from the cheapest single room in low sea-

son to the most expensive double in high season.

under 75 Euros
75-130 Euros
130-189 Euros
over 180 Euros

Prices have been calculated to include VAT and breakfast. (In some cases, the hotels already include breakfast in their standard rates; in others, they charge a hefty supplement. For reasons of comparability, we have taken this into account when placing the hotel within our price bands.)

In cases where hotels have suites available at a higher price, we have indicated this with an additional price band (e.g. L-LL - LLL). Prices for half board are per person and are indicated with the symbols (DB&B).

Prices for apartments are also calculated on the basis of cost per person, per day. Undoubtedly, these represent excellent value (especially for families) and normally fall within our lower price band. However, please remember that a full range of hotel services will not be available and that there are minimum-stay requirements, usually three days in low season and a week during the busy period. Full details of booking deposits can be obtained from the owners.

Caution Hotels, especially in Florence, sometimes charge more than their advertised rates in high season, when there is competition for rooms. Occasionally, you may find that the price asked is higher than that indicated by our price bands.
Rooms
Italian hotels can be exasperatingly vague on the number of rooms they have, especially in the more modest family-run establishments.

This may be a tax dodge (farmhouse bed-and-breakfasts are not supposed to have more than a certain number in order to benefit from financial concessions); it may also be a question of flexibility: a suite may be rented out as a standard double, or a three-day minimum stay waived in low season. It may be worth telephoning or faxing to ask for further details of rooms.

Facilities
We list public rooms plus outdoor and sporting facilities belonging to the hotel as well as any in the vicinity.

Credit cards
We use the following abbreviations for credit cards:

AE	American Express
DC	Diners Club
EC	Eurocard
MC	Master Card
V	Visa/Barclaycard/Bank Americard/Carte Bleue/Carta Si

Credit cards are now more widely accepted in Italy than before, with the exception of farmhouse bed-and-breakfasts, which prefer cash or travellers' cheques.

Children
Children are nearly always welcome in Italian hotels (and restaurants). Some hotels clearly wish to offer their guests plenty of peace and quiet, and therefore discourage too many mini-guests. Others generally offer discounts on third beds in the room.

Disabled
'No special facilities' is too frequent a comment under this heading, but understandable if you consider the buildings in which the hotels are located. Many of our entries are planning installation of special bathrooms and ramps for ease of access, but centuries-old buildings can prove intractable in these matters.

Closed
March to November is the important season for Tuscan and Umbrian hotels and many close for the winter months (except for a couple of weeks around Christmas and the New Year). In and near the main cities, hotels are open the whole year around to cater for domestic tourism and numerous congresses.

We list below Italy's official public holidays when banks and shops are shut and levels of public transport reduced. In Tuscany and Umbria, like the rest of the country, most towns have their own local holidays, usually the feast day of the patron saint, often celebrated with a fair and fireworks.

In addition to these are traditional events and festivals peculiar to each locality: Siena has its famous horse-race in Piazza del Campo (the Palio); in Arezzo, they joust in full medieval costumes; in Florence, they still play a lethal version of traditional football (calcio in costume); in Gubbio, teams of young men run up and down a steep mountain carrying gigantic wooden 'candles', apparently just for the fun of it. Religious pageantry is particularly rich around Easter and food and wine get their turn in the autumn with fairs ('sagre') devoted to tasting of local specialities: Chianti Classico, truffles (in Umbria), pecorino cheese (in the Pienza area), boar, and olive oil. Details can be had from local tourist offices, or keep an eye out for posters.

New Year's Day (Capodanno) Jan 1; Epiphany (Epifania) Jan 6; Holy Friday (Venerdí Santo); Easter Sunday (Pasqua); Easter Monday (Pasquetta); Liberation Day (Liberazione) April 25; May Day (Festa del Lavoro) May 1; Assumption of the Virgin (Ferragosto) Aug 15; All Saints' Day (Tutti Santi) Nov 1; Immaculate Conception (Immacolata Concezione) Dec 8; Christmas Day (Natale) Dec 25; St. Stephen's Day (Santo Stefano) Dec 26.

REPORTING TO THE GUIDE

Please write and tell us about your experiences of small hotels, guest-houses and inns, whether good or bad, whether listed in this edition or not. As well as hotels in Spain, we are interested in hotels in Britain and Ireland, Italy, France, Portugal, Austria, Switzerland, Germany and other European countries, and those in the eastern United States.

The address to write to is:

The Editor,
c/o Duncan Petersen Publishing Ltd,
31 Ceylon Road,
London W14 0PY.

Checklist
Please use a separate sheet of paper for each report; include your name, address and telephone number on each report.
Your reports will be received with particular pleasure if they are typed, and if they are organized under the following headings:

Name of establishment
Town or village it is in, or nearest
Full address, including post code
Telephone number
Time and duration of visit
The building and setting
The public rooms
The bedrooms and bathrooms
Physical comfort (chairs, beds, heat, light, hot water)

Standards of maintenance and housekeeping
Atmosphere, welcome and service
Food
Value for money

We assume that in writing you have no objections to your views being published unpaid, either verbatim or in an edited version. Names of major outside contributors are acknowledged, at the editor's discretion, in the guide.

Castelnuovo
di Garfagnana

Carrara

MASSA

1

Forte dei
Marmi

A12

Pietrasanta
75

Camaiore

Marina di
Pietrasanta

Viareggio

A11

Massarosa

A12

Santa Maria del Giudice
76

A11

Massa Azienda di
Promozione Turistica
Viale Vespucci 24
54037 Marina di Massa
Tel (0585) 240046
Fax (0585) 869015

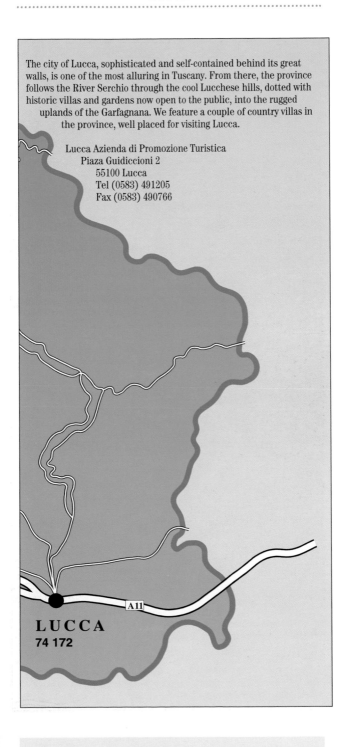

The city of Lucca, sophisticated and self-contained behind its great walls, is one of the most alluring in Tuscany. From there, the province follows the River Serchio through the cool Lucchese hills, dotted with historic villas and gardens now open to the public, into the rugged uplands of the Garfagnana. We feature a couple of country villas in the province, well placed for visiting Lucca.

Lucca Azienda di Promozione Turistica
Piaza Guidiccioni 2
55100 Lucca
Tel (0583) 491205
Fax (0583) 490766

A11

LUCCA
74 172

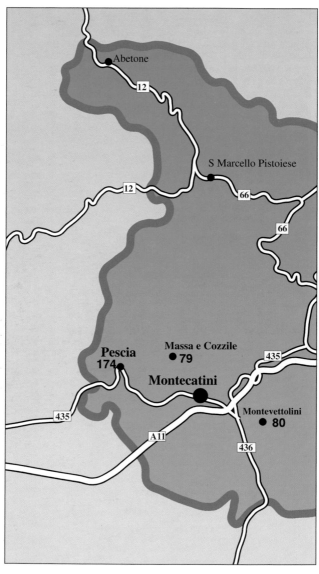

The little city of Pistoia, with its quintessential medieval square, its wealth of charming churches (containing three important early Renaissance pulpits) and its enchanting della Robbia frieze across the Ospedale del Ceppo, is one of the best-kept secrets in Tuscany. It has the added advantage of being a well-placed base for visiting Pisa, Lucca and Florence. The surrounding Pistoian hills are serenely peaceful, and we have several agreeable places to stay at in these hills, including self-catering apartments, bed-and-breakfasts and hotels proper, including one real gem.

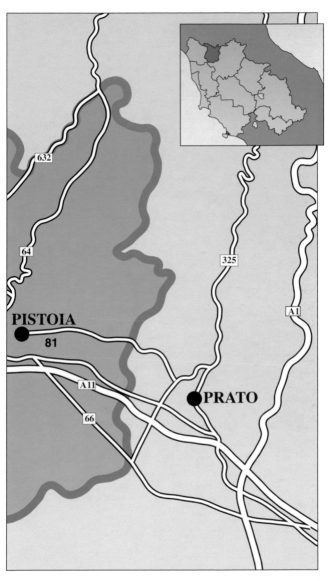

Pistoia Azienda di Promozione Turistica
Via Marconi 28
San Marcello Pistoiese
51028 Pistoia
Tel (0573) 630145
Fax (0573) 622120

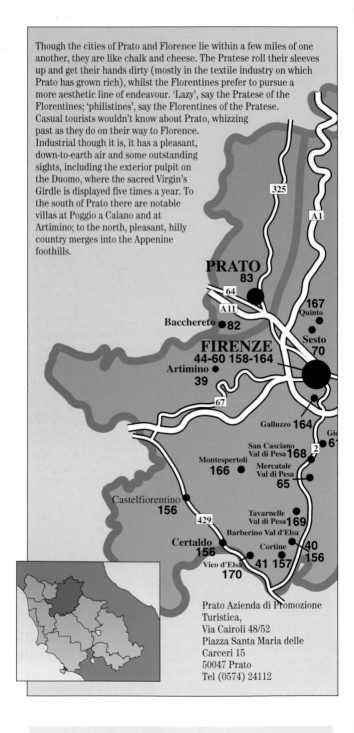

Though the cities of Prato and Florence lie within a few miles of one another, they are like chalk and cheese. The Pratese roll their sleeves up and get their hands dirty (mostly in the textile industry on which Prato has grown rich), whilst the Florentines prefer to pursue a more aesthetic line of endeavour. 'Lazy', say the Pratese of the Florentines; 'philistines', say the Florentines of the Pratese. Casual tourists wouldn't know about Prato, whizzing past as they do on their way to Florence. Industrial though it is, it has a pleasant, down-to-earth air and some outstanding sights, including the exterior pulpit on the Duomo, where the sacred Virgin's Girdle is displayed five times a year. To the south of Prato there are notable villas at Poggio a Caiano and at Artimino; to the north, pleasant, hilly country merges into the Appenine foothills.

325

A1

PRATO
83

64

A11

Bacchereto 82

167
Quinto

FIRENZE
44-60 158-164

Sesto
70

Artimino
39

67

Galluzzo 164

Gi
6

San Casciano
Val di Pesa 168

2

Montespertoli
166

Mercatale
Val di Pesa
65

Castelfiorentino
156

429

Tavarnelle
Val di Pesa 169

Barberino Val d'Elsa

Certaldo
156

Cortine

40
156

Vico d'Elsa
170

41 157

Prato Azienda di Promozione
Turistica,
Via Cairoli 48/52
Piazza Santa Maria delle
Carceri 15
50047 Prato
Tel (0574) 24112

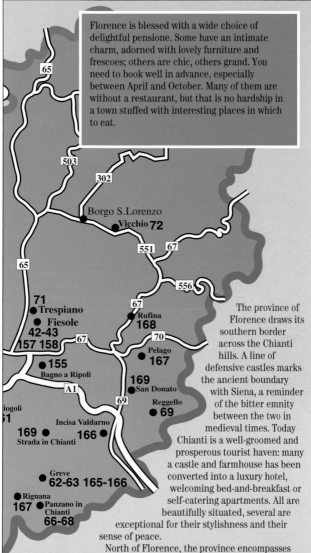

Florence is blessed with a wide choice of delightful pensione. Some have an intimate charm, adorned with lovely furniture and frescoes; others are chic, others grand. You need to book well in advance, especially between April and October. Many of them are without a restaurant, but that is no hardship in a town stuffed with interesting places in which to eat.

503

302

Borgo S.Lorenzo
Vicchio 72

551   67

65

556

71
●Trespiano
● Fiesole
42-43
157 158   67

● 155
Bagno a Ripoli
A1

iogoli
1

Incisa Valdarno
169 ●   166 ●
Strada in Chianti

● Greve
62-63 165-166

●Rignana
167 ●Panzano in
Chianti
66-68

67
Rufina
168

70
Pelago
167

169
San Donato
Reggello
● 69

The province of Florence draws its southern border across the Chianti hills. A line of defensive castles marks the ancient boundary with Siena, a reminder of the bitter emnity between the two in medieval times. Today Chianti is a well-groomed and prosperous tourist haven: many a castle and farmhouse has been converted into a luxury hotel, welcoming bed-and-breakfast or self-catering apartments. All are beautifully situated, several are exceptional for their stylishness and their sense of peace.

North of Florence, the province encompasses the lush and lovely region of the Mugello. Although it is just as beautiful as Chianti, its more modest tourist profile is reflected in the lack of good hotels. The immediate environs of Florence are better served; you can be on the edge of the city centre, yet staying in a hotel which feels almost completely remote.

Firenze Azienda di Promozione Turistica, Via Manzoni 16
50121 Firenze Tel (055) 23320 Fax (055) 2346286

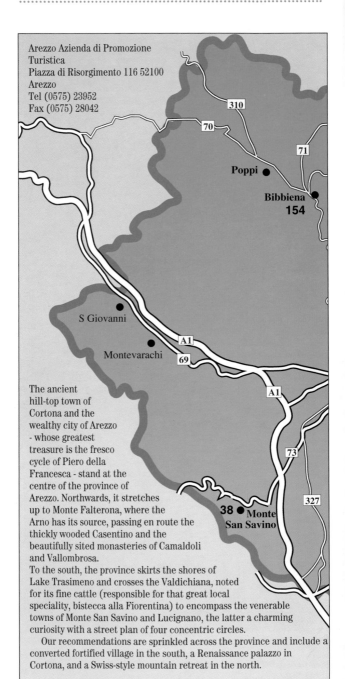

Arezzo Azienda di Promozione
Turistica
Piazza di Risorgimento 116 52100
Arezzo
Tel (0575) 23952
Fax (0575) 28042

310

70

71

Poppi ●

Bibbiena
154

●
S Giovanni

●
Montevarachi

A1

69

A1

73

327

The ancient
hill-top town of
Cortona and the
wealthy city of Arezzo
- whose greatest
treasure is the fresco
cycle of Piero della
Francesca - stand at the
centre of the province of
Arezzo. Northwards, it stretches
up to Monte Falterona, where the
Arno has its source, passing en route the
thickly wooded Casentino and the
beautifully sited monasteries of Camaldoli
and Vallombrosa.

38 ● Monte
San Savino

To the south, the province skirts the shores of
Lake Trasimeno and crosses the Valdichiana, noted
for its fine cattle (responsible for that great local
speciality, bistecca alla Fiorentina) to encompass the venerable
towns of Monte San Savino and Lucignano, the latter a charming
curiosity with a street plan of four concentric circles.

    Our recommendations are sprinkled across the province and include a
converted fortified village in the south, a Renaissance palazzo in
Cortona, and a Swiss-style mountain retreat in the north.

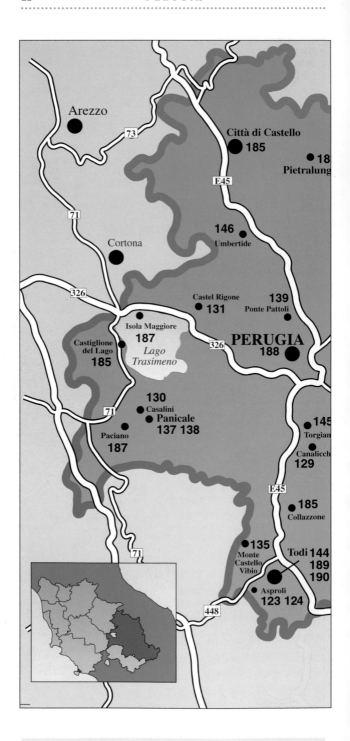

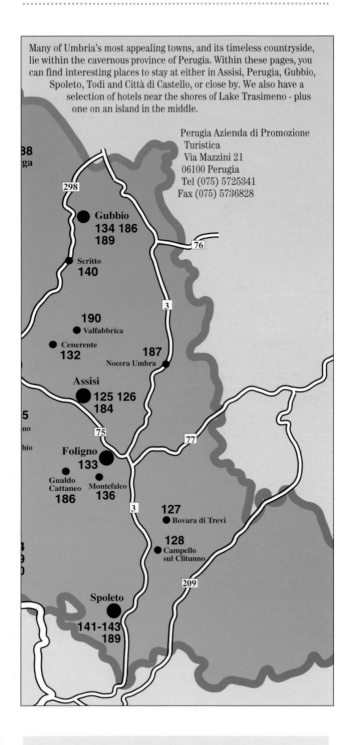

Many of Umbria's most appealing towns, and its timeless countryside, lie within the cavernous province of Perugia. Within these pages, you can find interesting places to stay at either in Assisi, Perugia, Gubbio, Spoleto, Todi and Città di Castello, or close by. We also have a selection of hotels near the shores of Lake Trasimeno - plus one on an island in the middle.

Perugia Azienda di Promozione
Turistica
Via Mazzini 21
06100 Perugia
Tel (075) 5725341
Fax (075) 5736828

88
ga

298

Gubbio
134 186
189

Scritto
140

76

190
Valfabbrica

Cenerente
132

3

187
Nocera Umbra

Assisi
125 126
184

5
no

hio

75

77

Foligno
133

Gualdo
Cattaneo   Montefalco
186   **136**

3

127
Bovara di Trevi

128
Campello
sul Clitunno

209

4
9
0

Spoleto

141-143
189

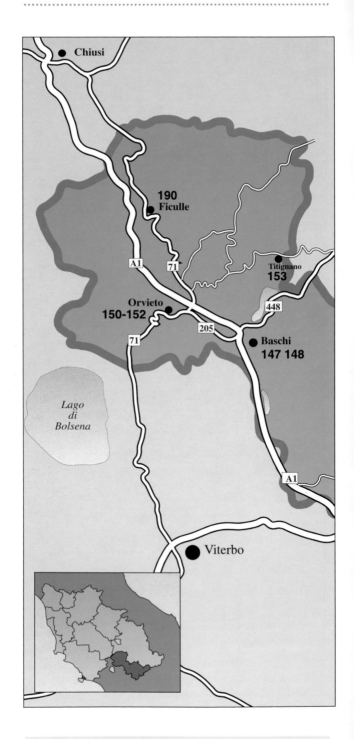

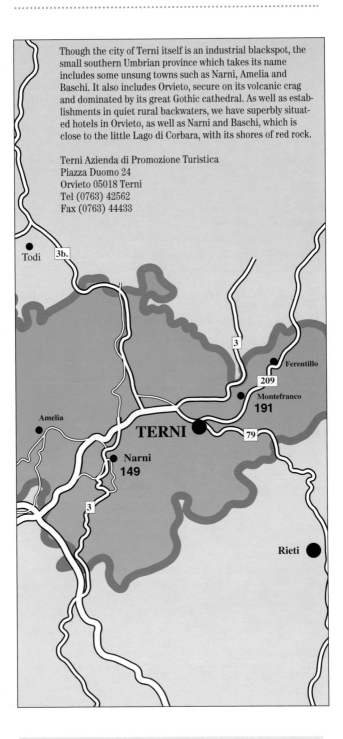

Though the city of Terni itself is an industrial blackspot, the small southern Umbrian province which takes its name includes some unsung towns such as Narni, Amelia and Baschi. It also includes Orvieto, secure on its volcanic crag and dominated by its great Gothic cathedral. As well as establishments in quiet rural backwaters, we have superbly situated hotels in Orvieto, as well as Narni and Baschi, which is close to the little Lago di Corbara, with its shores of red rock.

Terni Azienda di Promozione Turistica
Piazza Duomo 24
Orvieto 05018 Terni
Tel (0763) 42562
Fax (0763) 44433

Todi   3b.

3

Ferentillo
209
Montefranco
191

Amelia

TERNI   79

Narni
149

3

Rieti

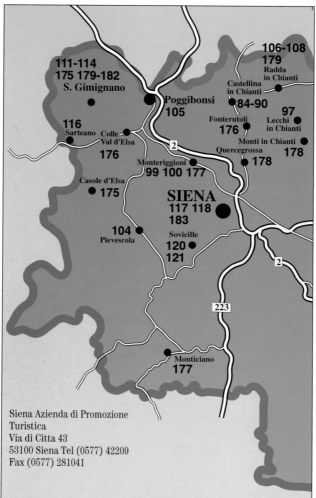

111-114
175 179-182
S. Gimignano

106-108
179
Radda
in Chianti

Castellina
in Chianti

Poggibonsi
105

84-90

116
Sarteano   Colle
Val d'Elsa

Fonterutoli
176

97
Lecchi
in Chianti

176

Monti in Chianti
Quercegrossa   **178**

178

Casole d'Elsa
175

Monteriggioni
99 100 177

SIENA
117 118
183

104
Pievescola

Sovicille
120
121

223

Monticiano
177

Siena Azienda di Promozione
Turistica
Via di Citta 43
53100 Siena Tel (0577) 42209
Fax (0577) 281041

The fair city of Siena stands at the centre of this geographically varied
province. To the east of Siena, the gentle vine-clad hills of Chianti give
way to the empty landscape of the Crete, and further south, to the Val
d'Orcia and the wooded slopes of Tuscany's highest mountain, Monte
Amiata. To the east of Siena is San Gimignano, whose bristling towers
and perfectly preserved medieval streets have made it into a hollow
tourist trap.

   Amongst our selection are the best of the farmhouses and castles
converted into stylish hotels which are now strewn across the Chianti
hills (others fall into the Firenze province, pages 18-19) as well as a
variety of accommodation in all corners of the region, and in the towns
of Siena, San Gimignano, Pienza and Monteriggioni.

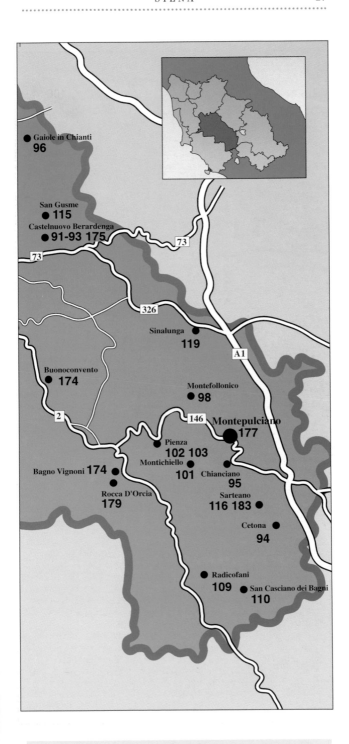

Gaiole in Chianti
96

San Gusme
115

Castelnuovo Berardenga
91-93 175

73

73

326

Sinalunga
119

A1

Buonoconvento
174

Montefollonico
98

2

146 Montepulciano
177

Pienza
102 103

Montichiello
101

Bagno Vignoni 174

Chianciano
95

Rocca D'Orcia
179

Sarteano
116 183

Cetona
94

Radicofani
109

San Casciano dei Bagni
110

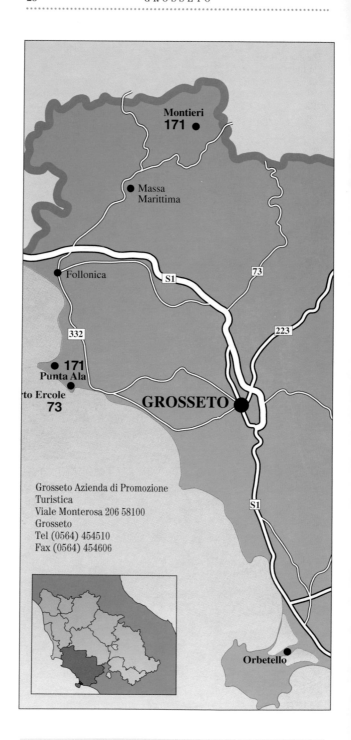

Grosseto Azienda di Promozione
Turistica
Viale Monterosa 206 58100
Grosseto
Tel (0564) 454510
Fax (0564) 454606

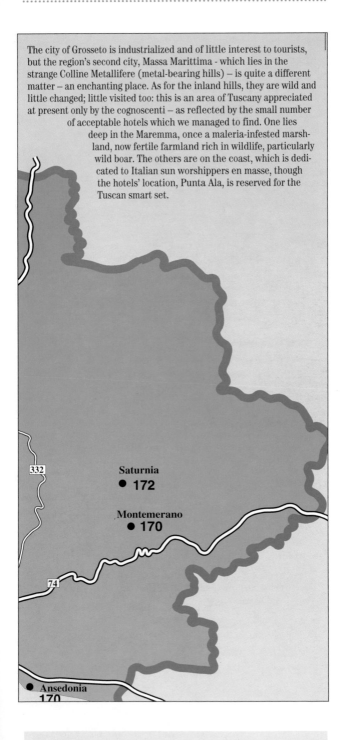

The city of Grosseto is industrialized and of little interest to tourists, but the region's second city, Massa Marittima - which lies in the strange Colline Metallifere (metal-bearing hills) – is quite a different matter – an enchanting place. As for the inland hills, they are wild and little changed; little visited too: this is an area of Tuscany appreciated at present only by the cognoscenti – as reflected by the small number of acceptable hotels which we managed to find. One lies deep in the Maremma, once a maleria-infested marshland, now fertile farmland rich in wildlife, particularly wild boar. The others are on the coast, which is dedicated to Italian sun worshippers en masse, though the hotels' location, Punta Ala, is reserved for the Tuscan smart set.

332

Saturnia
● 172

Montemerano
● 170

74

● **Ansedonia**
170

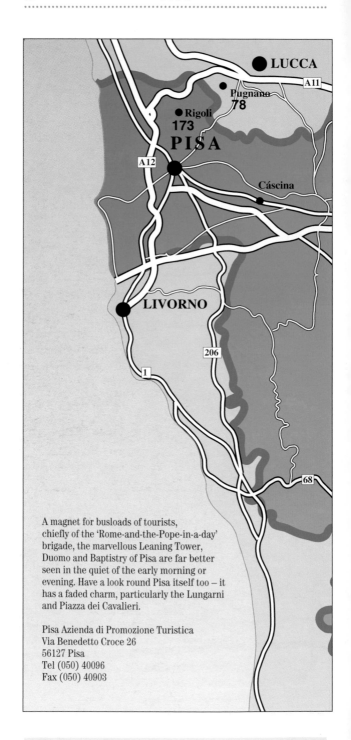

A magnet for busloads of tourists, chiefly of the 'Rome-and-the-Pope-in-a-day' brigade, the marvellous Leaning Tower, Duomo and Baptistry of Pisa are far better seen in the quiet of the early morning or evening. Have a look round Pisa itself too – it has a faded charm, particularly the Lungarni and Piazza dei Cavalieri.

Pisa Azienda di Promozione Turistica
Via Benedetto Croce 26
56127 Pisa
Tel (050) 40096
Fax (050) 40903

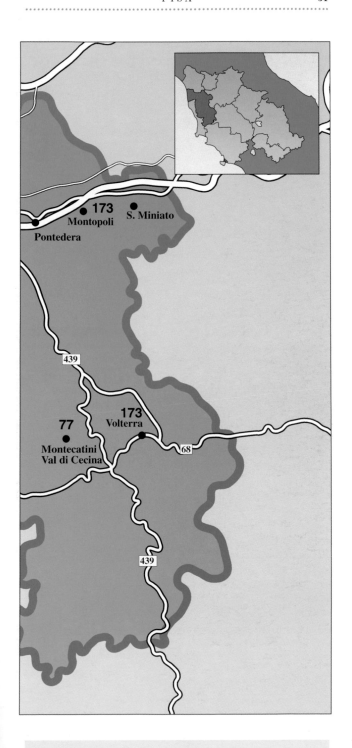

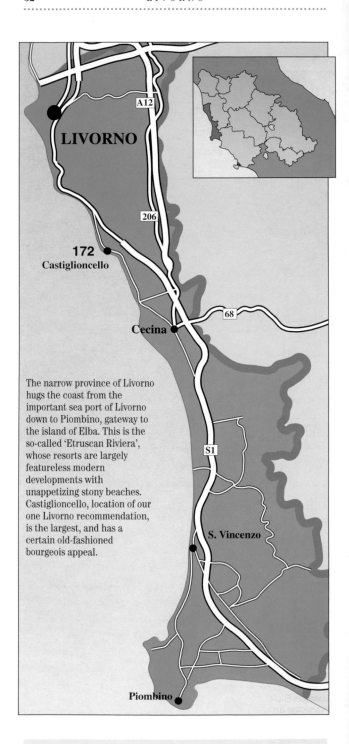

LIVORNO

A12

206

172
Castiglioncello

68

Cecina

S1

The narrow province of Livorno
hugs the coast from the
important sea port of Livorno
down to Piombino, gateway to
the island of Elba. This is the
so-called 'Etruscan Riviera',
whose resorts are largely
featureless modern
developments with
unappetizing stony beaches.
Castiglioncello, location of our
one Livorno recommendation,
is the largest, and has a
certain old-fashioned
bourgeois appeal.

S. Vincenzo

Piombino

AREZZO

CAPRESE MICHELANGELO

FONTE DELLA GALLETTA
~ MOUNTAIN HOTEL ~

Alpe Faggetta, Caprese Michelangelo, 52033 Arezzo
TEL & FAX (0575) 793925

A WINDING CLIMB through chestnut woods takes you up from the summer heat of the Tiber plain into the walkers' kingdom of the Alpe di Catinaia. At 800 m above sea level, the temperature here rarely reaches 30°C, even on the hottest July day.

The father of the present owners built this stone retreat some 30 years ago in a style that owes more to Switzerland than Tuscany. For most of the year (except weekends and August), it is a tranquil, almost forgotten place. This is its chief charm.

The modern bedrooms in the main building, refurbished in 1994, are small and rather anonymous, while the annexe rooms have been refurbished more recently. The beds are softly sprung, though the proprietor will place a board beneath the mattress if you prefer. Downstairs, the pine-tabled restaurant is anything but cosy. It does, however, offer a tempting range of local dishes according to season.

From the hotel, paths take you up through beech woods to the meadows of the Prate della Regina and the 1,400-m summit of Monte il Castello, with views of the Tiber and east to the Casentino.

~

NEARBY Michelangelo's birthplace at Caprese Michelangelo (6 km).
FOOD breakfastr, lunch, dinner
PRICE €
ROOMS 13 double in the hotel & 6 in separate ennexe.
FACILITIES restaurant, bar, sitting-room, garden,lake
CREDIT CARDS A, MC, V
CHILDREN accepted
DISABLED access possible
PETS not accepted
CLOSED 6 Jan to may (except weekends)
LANGUAGES English
PROPRIETORS Berlicchi family

AREZZO

CASTIGLION FIORENITO

VILLA SCHIATTI
~ COUNTRY VILLA ~

Località Montecchio, 131Castiglion Fiorentino, 52043 Arezzo
TEL (05750 651481 **FAX** 90575) 651482

SET AMONG OLIVE GROVES, this substantial Tuscan villa offers the space and simplicity of a family hotel with a number of apartments for longer-term guests. The Schiatti family built their two-towered villa between Castiglion Fiorentino and that most Tuscan of Tuscan hilltowns, Cortona, in the early years of the 19thC, but they lived here for barely a century before their line disappeared.

The present owners, the Bortot family, arrived in 1989 and set about restoring the villa with the minimum of interference to the original structure. Most of its stone and brick floors remain as they were, while the walls are whitewashed and its modest rooms are furnished with unobjectionable reproduction rustic furniture. The interior, however, lacks touches of thoughtful detail.

Signora Patrizia Bortot's quiet and friendly welcome – she speaks fluent English as well as German and French – and the reasonableness of the charges have helped to bring back an increasing number of guests each year. The evening meal, served at eight in the villa's rather impersonal dining-room, is simple and wholesome.

~

NEARBY Castiglion Fiorenito (3km); Cortona (8km).
LOCATION 5 km of Castiglion Fiorenito, 1 km above the SS71; with gardens and car parking
FOOD breakfast, dinner
PRICE (€)
ROOMS 9 double rooms with shower; three family apartments; all rooms have central heating, TV, phone
FACILITIES text
CREDIT CARDS EA, MC,V **CHILDREN** welcome
DISABLED access difficult **PETS** accepted
CLOSED Jan **LANGUAGES** English, French, German
PROPRIETORS Bordot family

AREZZO

AGRI SALOTTO
~ COUNTRY GUEST-HOUSE ~

Loc. Burcinella 88, Santa Caterina di Cortona, 52040 Arezzo
TEL (0575) 617417 **FAX** (0575) 617417

O N THE PLAIN of Valdichiana, below Cortona clinging to its hillside, can be found a type of farmhouse unique in Tuscany. Constructed during the 18thC when the area was part of the Grand Duchy of Tuscany, they are known as case leopoldiane. On the ground floors were the stables and store-rooms; upstairs were the living quarters and, rising above the main roof, a pigeon-loft. Sadly, many of these have fallen into disrepair over the years, but the Bianchis have made a fine job of restoring one of the few remaining.

On the ground floor is a light and airy, U-shaped space occupied by the restaurant and the sitting area where guests take their aperitivi and coffee on large, comfortable sofas. The essential austerity of the Tuscan rustic style has been softened by antique mirrors and deep blue Chinese vases. Most of the apartments are upstairs, spacious and bright, stylishly furnished with a mixture of old and new pieces. Prices are reasonable and overnight stays are possible (subject to availability in high season). A garden and large swimming-pool are at the disposal of guests, and the tranquillity of the surrounding countryside will make you want to prolong your stay.

~

NEARBY Cortona (10 km); Siena (54 km).
LOCATION in own grounds;ample car parking
FOOD dinner
PRICE ⑥⑥
ROOMS 5 apartments (1 two-person, 2 four-person, 2 six-person),all with bath or shower, phone,TV, living-room, kitchen
FACILITIES sitting-room,restaurant, laundry,garden, swimming-pool
CREDIT CARDS not accepted **CHILDREN** careful children only
DISABLED one adapted apartment **PETS** not accepted
CLOSED 3 weeks in Jan
LANGUAGES English, French
PROPRIETORS Silvana and Giovanni Bianchi

AREZZO

CORTONA

IL FALCONIERE
~ COUNTRY VILLA HOTEL ~

Loc. San Martino, Cortona, 52044 Arezzo
TEL (0575) 612 679 **FAX** (0575) 612 927

THE PLAIN SURROUNDING Lake Trasimeno over which Il Falconiere looks was once the scene of some of Hannibal's fiercest battles against the Romans, and many of the local place-names refer to bones and blood. Nowadays the only carnage takes place on the A1 autostrada (the Sunny Motorway) but Il Falconiere is such a haven of civilized living that you will never realize that you are only twenty minutes away from one of Italy's riskiest tourist experiences.

Reached through quiet country lanes just outside Cortona, the main villa (built in the 17thC around an earlier fortified tower) is set in land-scaped grounds of olives, rosemary hedges, fruit trees and roses, which also contain the old lemon house (now a top-class restaurant) and the still-functioning chapel with an adjoining suite. Meticulous attention has been given to every aspect of decoration and furnishing, from trompe-l'oeil number scrolls outside each room to the hand-embroidered window-hangings. Persian rugs rest easily on uneven, antique terracotta floors. In the pigeon-loft of the old tower, reached by a narrow, stone spiral staircase, is a small bedroom with an unsurpassed view of the Valdichiana.

~

NEARBY Cortona (3 km); Arezzo (29 km); Lake Trasimeno (10 km).
LOCATION just outside Cortona in its own grounds overlooking Valdichiana; ample parking
FOOD breakfast, lunch, dinner
PRICE €€-€€€€
ROOMS 10 double, 2 suites; all with bath or shower, air-conditioning, minibar, phone, TV, safe
FACILITIES swimming-pool (May-Sep only), gardens, restaurant
CREDIT CARDS AE, DC, V
CHILDREN welcome **DISABLED** no special facilities
PETS yes but not in rooms
CLOSED 6 Jan to mid-Feb
LANGUAGES English, French, German
PROPRIETORS Riccardo Baracchi and Silvia Regi

AREZZO

CORTONA

SAN MICHELE
∼ TOWN HOTEL ∼

Via Guelfa 15, Cortona, 52044 Arezzo
TEL (0575) 604348 **FAX** (0575) 630147

IT MIGHT SOUND like an easy matter to turn a fine Renaissance palace into a hotel of character, but we have seen too many examples of good buildings brutalised by excessive and unwanted luxury, over-modernization and an almost wilful blindness to the original style, not to be delighted when the job has been properly done.

The Hotel San Michele has not fluffed the opportunites offered by the former seat of the Etruscan Academy, but has steered a precise course between the twin dangers of unwarranted adventurousness and lame timidity. White plaster and stark beams are complemented with rich modern fabrics; sofas of the finest leather are strewn about terracotta floors that seem glazed with some rich wax. Carefully-placed lights emphasize the gracefully interlocking curves of the cortile. The common rooms are full of such stylish features as frescoed friezes and immense carved stone fireplaces.

The bedrooms are more modest in style, with wrought-iron beds and rustic antiques, and in need of refurbishment according to a recent report. Some of the more spacious ones have an extra mezzanine to provide separate sleeping and sitting areas.

∼

NEARBY Diocesan Museum, Arezzo (29 km); Perugia (51 km).
LOCATION 16th C. palazzo in middle of town; garage nearby
FOOD breakfast only
PRICE €€€
ROOMS 40 double, all with bath or shower; TV, phone, minibar
FACILITIES garage, sitting-room, breakfast-room, conference-room
CREDIT CARDS AE, DC, MC, V
CHILDREN welcome
DISABLED one suitable room
PETS small dogs **CLOSED** 15 Jan-6 Mar
LANGUAGES English, French, German **PROPRIETOR** Paopo Alunno

AREZZO

MONTE SAN SAVINO

CASTELLO DI GARGONZA
∿ HILLTOP CASTLE ∿

Gargonza, Monte San Savino, 52048 Arezzo
TEL (0575) 847021/22/23 **FAX** (0575)847054

A TREE-LINED ROAD sweeps up the hill alongside the castle walls and brings you into the main square of this fortress-village, dominated by a stately crenellated tower where in more dangerous days look-outs surveyed the Valdichiana below for signs of approaching enemies. The village is as it was centuries ago, a jumble of stone houses connected by crooked paths. Traffic is not allowed in the castle area (except for loading and unloading baggage) and there is a hushed silent atmosphere which at night seems almost eerie – but don't let that put you off.

Most of the accommodation is given over to apartments in 19 picturesque houses, each with its own name, available for weekly rentals (occasionally for less), sleeping from two to seven persons. They make ideal choices for families. Overnight stays are available in the guest-house next to the reception. The rooms are simple.

At the bottom of the hill is the Torre di Gargonza restaurant of which we have mixed reports. The grounds have recently been improved and there is a new swimming-pool next door. Reports would be welcome.

∿

NEARBY Siena (35 km); Arezzo (25 km).
LOCATION 8 km W of Monte San Savino, off the SS 73; car parking outside the castle
FOOD breakfast, lunch, dinner
PRICE €€–€€€
ROOMS 6 double, 1 triple, all with bath or shower, phone; 25 self-catering apartments with 1 to 4 bedrooms
FACILITIES 4 sitting-rooms (2 for meetings), bar, restaurant, swimming-pool, bowls
CREDIT CARDS AE, DC, EC, MC, V
CHILDREN welcome
DISABLED not suitable
PETS small dogs **CLOSED** 3 weeks in Nov and Jan
LANGUAGES English, French, some German
PROPRIETOR Conte Roberto Guicciardini

FIRENZE

ARTIMINO

PAGGERIA MEDICEA
~ COUNTRY HOTEL ~

Viale Papa Giovanni XXIII, Artimino, 59015 Firenze
TEL (055) 871 8081 **FAX** (055) 871 80870
E-MAIL artimino@tin.it **WEBSITE** www.artimino.it

VILLA ARTIMINO, a Medici villa built when the family was at the height of its powers, stands high in the hills of the wine-producing district of Carmignano, west of Florence. Money from their banking activities and a sense of style that made them the greatest ever patrons of the arts combined to make this one of their most magnificent country residences. The villa is now a museum, but the former stables are an excellent hotel.

They certainly did their grooms well. Both sides of the long, low building are flanked by beautifully articulated loggias on to which most of the bedrooms open. The rooms themselves are spacious and shadily cool in summer; in other seasons, visitors may find that the loggia prevents enough light from getting in. Each has a large stone fireplace so that the roof, like the villa's beside, is cluttered with chimneys standing to attention like toy soldiers.

Downstairs, the stalls have been turned into breakfast-rooms and sitting areas full of comfortable couches, interesting books, old rugs and prints. The gardens look on to the city simmering on the sultry plain below and, even in July, catch a cool evening breeze.

~

NEARBY Prato (15 km); Florence (24 km); Etruscan museum.
LOCATION 24 km NW of Florence, with car parking
FOOD breakfast, lunch, dinner
PRICE €€
ROOMS 36 double, some with bath, most with shower;
1 single with shower; all have central heating, air-condit-ioning, minibar, TV, phone, radio; 43 apartments in Artimino village
FACILITIES breakfast-room, sitting-room, TV room, restaurant, 2 tennis-courts, jogging, swimming-pool, mountain bikes, laundry
CREDIT CARDS AE, DC, MC, V
CHILDREN welcome**DISABLED** some rooms accessible
PETS accepted **CLOSED** never **LANGUAGES** English, French
MANAGER Alessandro Gualtie

FIRENZE

IL PARETAIO
~ COUNTRY GUEST-HOUSE ~

San Filippo, Barberino Val d'Elsa, 50021 Firenze
TEL (055) 50021 **FAX** (055) 8059231

A GREAT ADDRESS for those interested in horse-riding but not to be dismissed by travellers in search of the country life. Strategically located between Florence and Siena, in hilly surroundings, Il Paretaio is a 17thC stone-built farmhouse on its own large estate.

The accommodation is simple but attractive. The ground-floor entrance and sitting area was originally a work-room, and still retains the old stone paving. A huge brick arch spans the central space and brick-vaulting contrasts with the plain white walls. Upstairs, the rustic style is continued in the exposed-beam ceilings and worn terracotta floors.

The dining-room is particularly attractive with its larch-wood table, ten feet long, where communal meals are served, and a huge open fireplace. Most of the bedrooms are off this room, with country furniture and equestrian prints. The most attractive bedroom is in the dovecot, a mini-tower at the top of the house with pretty little arched windows on three sides looking on to the rolling landscape.

Outside is a riding arena, and a swimming-pool.

~

NEARBY Florence (33 km); San Gimignano (21 km); Siena (34 km).
LOCATION 3 km S of Barberino Val d'Elsa
FOOD breakfast, dinner
PRICE €
ROOMS 6 double; two apartments for 4-5 people; reductions for children
FACILITIES garden, swimming-pool, horse-riding, (all standards and all ages), mountain bikes
CREDIT CARDS not accepted
CHILDREN welcome
DISABLED no special facilities
PETS accepted **CLOSED** never
LANGUAGES English, French
PROPRIETORS Giovanni and Cristina de Marchi

FIRENZE

CORTINE

LA CHIARA DI PRUMIANO
~ FARM GUEST-HOUSE ~

Strada di Cortine 12, 50021 Barberino Val d'Elsa, Firenze
TEL (055) 8075583 **FAX** (055) 8075678
E-MAIL prumiano@tin.it

WHEN FOUR FAMILIES bought the Chiara di Prumiano (formerly a country residence of the Corsini family) some 15 years ago with plans to make it pay for itself, they took on an enormous project. The estate runs to 40 hectares of land with a grand, albeit rather crumbling, villa at the centre of a small hamlet, complete with its own tiny chapel.

Now run by two of the original owners, the Chiara is a successful business, but the atmosphere is laid-back and alternative. The creeper-clad villa offers modestly furnished but spacious bedrooms, a sitting-room of baronial proportions, two dining rooms and various spaces used for seminars and workshops. Other accommodation is in simple, tastefully converted buildings nearby.

Courses are hosted year-round, so the guest may find himself or herself eating at one of the long, communal tables with a Yoga group. The delicious meals are predominantly (but not exclusively) vegetarian and make creative use of home-grown fruit and vegetables, olive oil and wine.

~

NEARBY Siena (40 km); San Gimignano (25 km); Florence (35 km).
LOCATION 4 km SE of Barberino; best approached from the San Donato superstrada exit
FOOD breakfast; lunch and dinner on request
PRICE €
ROOMS 15 doubles and 2 apartments, 11 with bath or shower.
FACILITIES meeting rooms, garden, swimming pool, riding
CREDIT CARDS EC, MC, V **CHILDREN** welcome
DISABLED access difficult
PETS accepted but please advise when booking
CLOSED Christmas-mid Ja
LANGUAGES English, French, Spanish
PROPRIETORS Gaia Mezzadri and Antonio Pescett

FIRENZE

FIESOLE

LE CANELLI
~ TOWN GUEST-HOUSE ~

Via Gramsci 52/54/56, 50014 Fiesole, Florence
TEL (055) 5978336 **FAX** (055) 5978292
E-MAIL info @lecannelli.com **WEBSITE** www.lecannelli.com

HERE IS THAT RARITY, a new discovery, not featured in other guides (or not yet). The proprietors, Sara and Simona Corsi, have a father with a building business, so who better to restore these two old town houses on Fiesole's main street, a little way north of the main square. Once finished, he handed over the management of the little bed-and-breakfast to his two daughters, who have enthusiastically set about their new activity since opening in November 1999.

The cool hills surrounding Fiesole are studded with spectacular villas, and many of the hotels in the area are correspondingly expensive. Il Trebbiolo, one of our recommendations some distance outside Fiesole, has closed; so we are all the more pleased to include Le Cannelli as a low-cost, but charming, alternative. It has been carefully decorated in simple, yet comfortable style. Bedrooms are quite spacious, and one even has a duplex with two single beds up top. Two offer lovely views of the hills to the north. Those on the somewhat noisy street have double glazing. The blue-and-white bathrooms are spotless. The pretty room where Sara and Simona prepare breakfast is unfortunately right on the street.

~

NEARBY Florence (8 km); Roman amphitheatre.
LOCATION on main street north of main square
FOOD breakfast
PRICE €–€€€
ROOMS 1 single, 2 doubles, 1 triple, 1 family room, all with bath or shower, phone, TV, air-conditioning
FACILITIES breakfast room
CREDIT CARDS AE, DC, EC, MC, V
CHILDREN welcome
DISABLED not suitable
CLOSED two months in winter
LANGUAGES English, French
PROPRIETORS Sara and Simona Corsi

FIRENZE

FIESOLE

VILLA SAN MICHELE
~ CONVERTED MONASTERY ~

Via di Doccia 4, Fiesole, 50014 Firenze
TEL (055) 59451 **FAX** (055) 598734 **E MAIL** reservations@villasanmichele.net
WEB SITE www.orient/expresshotels.com

A HOTEL SO EXPENSIVE that even its cheapest single rooms, which are rather small, lie well outside the price range represented by our symbols: one of the better suites will cost you nearly three million lire, enough to pay dinner for at least ten people at Florence's finest restaurant. At these prices one expects transcendent perfection, but we have the feeling that part of the frisson of staying at San Michele is having paid so much in the first place.

Cost aside, the hotel is undoubtedly among the finest in the guide, both for its location, and for the character of its buildings, whose post-war restoration has been successful in removing some insensitive 19thC embellishments and repairing bomb damage. The dignified façade with its porticoed loggia is based on a design attributed to Michaelangelo, and once you pass through the doors you have the odd sensation of checking-in to a former church. Antiques, acquired without heed of expense, abound, although there is also some modern furniture. Bedrooms in the new annex have less character than those in the original building. The chic restaurant serves meals on a lovely, covered lemon terrace.

~

NEARBY Florence (6 km); Fiesole (1 km).
LOCATION just below Fiesole; own car parking
FOOD breakfast, lunch, dinner
PRICE €€€€
ROOMS 25 double, 15 suites, all with bath and shower, phone, TV, heating, air-conditioning
FACILITIES sitting-rooms, bar, restaurant, terrace, swimming-pool, private city bus shuttle
SMOKING allowed **CREDIT CARDS** AE, DC, EC, MC, V **CHILDREN** welcome
DISABLED one suitable room **PETS** small dogs only (not in restaurant or near pool)
CLOSED end-Nov to mid-Mar
LANGUAGES English, French, German, Spanish
MANAGER Maurizio Saccani

FIRENZE

FLORENCE

ANNALENA
~ TOWN GUEST-HOUSE ~

Via Romana 34, 50125 Firenze
TEL (055) 222402/3 **FAX** (055) 222402/3

ONE OF FLORENCE's traditional pensioni, still very much in the old style, with a regular clientèle. The Annalena is located opposite the Boboli gardens (the famous park laid out by Medici dukes) and many of the rooms look out on to a horticultural centre next door. Luckily, none of them has windows on the busy Via Romana.

The palazzo is said to be 15thC, belonging at one point to a young noble-woman, Annalena, whose tragic love story and early widowhood led her to withdraw from the world and give over her property as a place of retirement for other young widows. Since then, the palazzo has been offering hospitality of one sort or another, and during the war gave refuge to many foreigners in flight from Mussolini's police.

The tradition of hospitality continues to this day, and while the Annalena is no luxury hotel, it offers solid comforts not without hints of style at reasonable prices, with an owner attentive to his guests' needs. A huge salon now serves as reception, sitting-room, breakfast-room and bar. Bedrooms vary in size and bathrooms are acceptable.

~

NEARBY Palazzo Pitti, Ponte Vecchio, Palazzo Vecchio, Uffizi.
LOCATION \3 minutes' walk from Palazzo Pitti on S side of river; pay car parking nearby (20,000 lire approx.)
FOOD breakfast
PRICE ⓔⓔ–ⓔⓔⓔ
ROOMS 4 single, 16 double, all with bath or shower, phone, TV
FACILITIES sitting-room, bar breakfast-room, terrace
CREDIT CARDS AE, DC, EC, MC, V
CHILDREN welcome
DISABLED no special faciities
PETS accepted **CLOSED** never
LANGUAGES English, French, Greek
PROPRIETOr Claudio Salvestrini

FIRENZE

FLORENCE

CLASSIC
~ TOWN HOTEL ~

Viale Machiavelli 25, 50125 Florence
Tel (055) 229351/229352 **Fax** (055) 229353

STANDING IN ITS OWN LUSH GARDEN and rubbing shoulders with some of the most impressive residences in Florence, this pink-washed villa is on a leafy avenue just five minutes from Porta Romana, the old gate into the south of the city. A private residence until 1991, the house was rescued from decay and turned into a comfortable and friendly hotel which maintains admirably reasonable prices.

Bedrooms vary in size, but all are fairly spacious with parquet floors, original plasterwork, antique furniture and pretty bedspreads. Two have frescoes, and another hosts an impressive fireplace. The high ceilings on the first floor allow for a duplex arrangement with extra space for beds or sitting areas on a higher level while top-floor rooms have sloping, beamed attic ceilings and air-conditioning. A romantic annexe suite tucked away in the garden, complete with tiny kitchen area, offers extra privacy for the same price as a standard double.

In warmer weather, breakfast is served outside under a pergola, but even in winter the conservatory allows for a sunny - possibly even a warm - start to the day.

~

NEARBY Pitti Palace, Piazzale Michelangelo, Museo La Specola.
LOCATION In residential area five minutes' walk from Porta Romana; own car parking
FOOD breakfast
PRICE €–€€€€
ROOMS 1 single, 10 doubles/twins, 3 suites all with bath or shower, phone, TV; top floor rooms have air conditioning
FACILITIES breakfast room, garden, conservatory
CREDIT CARDS AE, DC, EC, MC, V
CHILDREN welcome **DISABLED** lift; ground-floor bedrooms
PETS permitted **CLOSED** 2 weeks in August
LANGUAGES English, French, German
PROPRIETOR Corinne Kraft

FIRENZE

FLORENCE

GALLERY, ART HOTEL
~ TOWN HOTEL ~

Vicolo del' Oro 5, 50120 Florence
TEL (055) 27263 **FAX** (055) 268557
E MAIL galleryhotel@lungarnohotels.com **WEB SITE** www.lungarnohotels.it

IT WAS NO PROBLEM to stretch our normal size limit to include Florence's newest hotel: first because it is unique, and second because it feels like a much smaller place. In a quiet piazzetta just a few steps from the Ponte Vecchio, the Gallery is a temple of contemporary design, a combination of east and west which provides endless curiosities to look at and to touch. While the style is minimalist, it avoids being cold. Colours are muted and restful. Greys, creams, taupes and white dominate, while dark African wood is used throughout to add warmth and contrast. Contemporary art hangs on the walls. There is an impressive feeling of space in the public rooms.

A smart bar with squashy sofas houses a large video screen, while the reading room is dominated by a huge bookcase filled with interesting volumes to be browsed through at leisure. Inviting knee rugs are draped over the pale sofas, almost begging the guest to relax with a book.

Bedrooms vary in size, but are all along the same stylish, sober lines. The bathrooms, with classic chrome fittings, are splendid.

~

NEARBY Ponte Vecchio, Pitti Palace, Uffizi.
LOCATION in centre of town next to Ponte Vecchio with valet car parking nearby
FOOD breakfast, light lunch, dinner
PRICE €€€€
ROOMS 60 doubles and f suites, all with bath or shower, phone, TV, air-conditioning, hair drier, safe
FACILITIES library, bar break-fast room, terrace
CREDIT CARDS AE, DC, EC, MC, V
CHILDREN welcome
DISABLED 2 adapted rooms
PETS small dogs accepted
CLOSED never
LANGUAGES English, French, German, Spanish, Japanese
GENERAL MANAGER Nedo Naldini

FIRENZE

FLORENCE

HELVETIA & BRISTOL
~ TOWN HOTEL ~

Via dei Pescioni 2, 50123 Firenze
TEL (055) 287814 **FAX** (055) 288353
E MAIL information-hbf@charminghotels.it

T HE HELVETIA was originally a Swiss-owned hotel right in the centre of
Florence which added the name Bristol to attract 19thC British travellers. After 1945, it gradually fell into decay until new management took
it over and began restoration in 1987, sparing no expense in their imaginative recreation of a 19thC luxury hotel.

Those with classical tastes, used to the stark simplicity of the Tuscan
style, may find the results cloying and indigestible, but others will enjoy
the rich colour schemes and heavy, dark antiques. The restaurant is undeniably elegant and hung with two amazing Art Nouveau lamps shaped like
shells and rocks. The least overwhelming room is a 1920s winter-garden,
full of handsome cane furniture and potted palms, with a green-tinted
glass ceiling. The bedrooms are, if anything, even more ornate than the
public rooms. Antiques, Venetian mirrors and chandeliers add to the opu-
lence. One of the finest features of the hotel is its extensive collection of
prints and pictures. Staff and service are smooth and professional. In 2000
the hotel extends into the next-door building, adding 18 new doubles and
three suites.

~

NEARBY Ponte Vecchio, Uffizi, Palazzo Vecchio, Palazzo Pitti.
LOCATION in the centre of town, opposite Palazzo Strozzi, W of Piazza Repubblica;
pay car parking nearby
FOOD breakfast, lunch, dinner
PRICE €€€€–€€€€€
ROOMS 9 single, 20 double, 20 suites, all with bath or shower, phone, TV, minibar,
air-conditioning
FACILITIES sitting-rooms, restaurant, bar, winter-garden
CREDIT CARDS AE, DC, EC, MC, V
CHILDREN welcome **DISABLED** some facilities
PETS small dogs **CLOSED** never
LANGUAGES English, French, German, Spanish
MANAGER Pietro Panelli

FIRENZE

FLORENCE

HERMITAGE
∽ TOWN GUEST-HOUSE ∽

Vicolo Marzio 1, Piazza del Pesce, 50122 Firenze
TEL (055) 287216 **FAX** (055) 212208
E-MAIL florence@hermitagehotel.com **WEBSITE** http://www.hermitagehotel.com

A HOTEL YOU ARE HARDLY LIKELY to stumble across, despite its central location next to the Ponte Vecchio on the north side of the Arno. A discreetly placed entrance in a small alley-way, opposite the porticos supporting Vasari's corridor, admits you to a lift taking you up five floors to the reception and its friendly, international staff.

The Hermitage is like a cappuccino: the best bits are on top and matters become more mundane as you descend. The roof terrace, filled with flowers in terracotta pots, shade provided by a pergola, commands unrivalled views of the city. Sitting there at breakfast, you can plan the day's excursions almost without the aid of a map. In case of bad weather, there is a light and airy breakfast-room on the fifth floor with a covered veranda. Next door is the sitting-room (and bar) looking directly on to the Ponte Vecchio and the Oltrarno, with comfortable couches. Bedrooms combine fairly successfully modern and old-fashioned furniture. After the Uffizi bombing in 1993, the streets around were banned to traffic, so noise is not a problem – assisted by the judicious, although not always sufficient, double-glazing on the busier riverside aspect.

∽

NEARBY Ponte Vecchio, Uffizi, Palazzo Vecchio, Palazzo Pitti, Duomo.
LOCATION right beside the Ponte Vecchio; private pay car parking nearby
FOOD breakfast
PRICE €€€€–€€€€€
ROOMS 3 single, 28 double, all with bath and/or shower; all rooms have central heating, air-conditioning
phone, satellite TV
FACILITIES sitting-room, bar, breakfast-room, roof-garden
CREDIT CARDS V, MC, EC **CHILDREN** welcome
DISABLED not suitable **PETS** accepted **CLOSED** never
LANGUAGES English, German, Portuguese
PROPRIETOR Vincenzo Scarcelli

FIRENZE

FLORENCE

J AND J
~ TOWN HOTEL ~

Via di Mezzo 20, 50121 Firenze
TEL (055) 2345005 **FAX** (055) 240282

THIS HIGHLY INDIVIDUAL hotel in a former convent of the 16thC is to be found, off the usual tourist routes, in a residential part of the old city centre. However, it is still convenient for visiting all the obligatory Florentine museums, with the advantage of peace and quiet when you get back to the hotel in the evening.

Perhaps it was the owner's training as an architect that gave him the confidence to combine old and new so strikingly in the decoration and furnishings. The building is, in fact, two, separated by a terracotta-paved cloister where breakfast is served during the summer months. In front of this, is a lovely light room with painted wicker furniture and a decorated vaulted ceiling, separated from the cloister only by the glassed-in arches. The sitting-room next door combines original features with pale modern furniture and mellow lighting.

Some of the bedrooms are enormous, possibly because they used to be studio flats, and could sleep a family of four in comfort. Each one is different in style, furnished with antiques and hand-woven fabrics. The character of the building does not allow for a lift.

~

NEARBY Santa Croce, San Marco, Santissima Annunziata.
LOCATION a few minutes' walk E of the Duomo
FOOD breakfast only
PRICE €€€€
ROOMS 18 double, two family rooms, all with bath or shower, phone, TV, minibar, air-conditioning
FACILITIES sitting-room, breakfast-room, courtyard
SMOKING permitted
CREDIT CARDS AE, DC, EC, MC, V
CHILDREN welcome **DISABLED** no special facilities
PETS not accepted **CLOSED** never
LANGUAGES English, French, German
PROPRIETOR James Cavagnari

FIRENZE

FLORENCE

LOGGIATO DEI SERVITI
~ TOWN HOTEL ~

Piazza SS. Annunziata 3, 50122 Firenze
TEL (055) 289 592/3/4 **FAX** (055) 289595
E MAIL loggiato_serviti@italyhotel.com **Web site** www.venere.it/firenze/loggiato_serviti

CHOICE OF ACCOMMODATION in the centre of Florence always presents the visitor with a dilemma: stylish establishments cost so much you feel that you should spend the entire day indoors, getting value for your money, while budget pensioni have the opposite effect. In our first edition, we said that none strikes the balance so well as Loggiato dei Serviti. Now, sadly, we have to qualify this by the fact that the piazza where the hotel stands is frequented by drug addicts. That aside, the Piazza Santissima Annunziata is Florence's most beautiful square. New, strict traffic regulations mean that the piazza no longer looks like a car park (however, it is difficult to get to the Loggiato by car) and one can now enjoy the full beauty of its elegant colonnades and equestrian statue.

The hotel is on the side opposite Brunelleschi's Ospedale degli Innocenti, underneath a portico decorated with ceramic medallions by della Robbia. The interior is cool and restrained; rooms are furnished with antiques and well-chosen modern pieces, some looking on to the piazza, others on to gardens behind. The pleasant ground-floor breakfast-room has softly playing opera.

~

NEARBY SS. Annunziato and San Marco; Accademia museum.
LOCATION five minute's walk from the Duomo, in quiet piazza; pay car parking in garage nearby
FOOD breakfast
PRICE €€€€–€€€€
ROOMS 19 double, 6 single, 4 suites, all with bath or shower, phone, TV, radio, safe, air-conditioning
FACILITIES breakfast-room, bar
CREDIT CARDS AE, DC, EC, MC, V **CHILDREN** text
DISABLED not suitable
PETS please check first
CLOSED never
LANGUAGES English, French **PROPRIETOR** Rodolfo Buttini Gattai

FIRENZE

FLORENCE

MONNA LISA
∼ TOWN HOTEL ∼

Borgo Pinti 27, 50121 Firenze
Tel (055) 2479751Fax (055) 2479755
E MAIL monnalis@ats.it **WEB SITE** www.monnalisa.it

THE ENTRANCE is as discreet as the hotel itself: at the back of a covered area opening into the palazzo from Borgo Pinti, used in bygone days for parking the padrone's horse-and-carriage, is a small door leading into this intriguing hotel.

A maze of rooms occupies the ground floor with Doric and Corinthian columns of pietra serena supporting heavy, decorated wooden ceilings. Light floods in from the back through leaded windows that give on to the garden. Old terracotta floors, dark and shiny from centuries of wax polish, lead the eye easily from one room to another. The family's collection of paintings and sculpture (including the original model for Giambologna's Rape of the Sabine Women) give a pleasant cluttered air to the public areas.

The garden is a definite plus in this claustrophobic city, so short of quiet, shady places in which to sit. Breakfast can be taken here in fine weather. Some of the bedrooms, in heavy, ornate style, have small terraces overlooking this delightful green haven.

One caution: we've had reports that reception can be somewhat cool. Reports from readers would be appreciated.

∼

NEARBY Cathedral, Santissima Annunziata, San Marco, Santa Croce.
LOCATION 5 minutes' walk E of the Duomo; pay car parking nearby
FOOD breakfast
PRICE €€€-€€€€
ROOMS 30 double, 5 single, all with bath or shower, phone, TV, minibar, heating, air-conditioning
FACILITIES sitting-rooms, bar, garden, private parking in Via della Pergola
CREDIT CARDS AE, DC, EC, MC, V
CHILDREN welcome **DISABLED** one adapted room
PETS accepted **CLOSED** never
LANGUAGES English, French, German **PROPRIETOR** Agostino Cona

FIRENZE

FLORENCE

MORANDI ALLA CROCETTA
～ TOWN GUEST-HOUSE ～

Via Laura 50, 50121 Firenze
TEL (055) 2344747 **FAX** (055) 2480954
E MAIL *hmorandi@dada.it* **WEB SITE** *www.hotelmorandi.it*

MORANDI ALLA CROCETTA, a family-run pensione occupying an apartment in the university part of town in a road leading to Piazza Santissima Annunziata. The entrance looks like any other on the street, without any neon signs, and you must ring a bell to be admitted. Reserve and discretion are the hallmarks here.

Quiet, tasteful interiors greet visitors in the second-floor apartment. The polished wooden floors, with strategically placed oriental carpets, echo the beamed ceilings and their decorated corbels. Architectural details are picked out in brick, and the white walls carry only a very few paintings and portraits. There is a small, intimate breakfast-room. All is impeccably maintained.

The bedrooms, quiet and comfortable, are furnished with antiques and some well-chosen modern pieces. Two of them have small terraces opening on to a small garden and another has the remains of 17thC frescoes depicting the life and works of Sister Domenica del Paradiso, founder of the original convent. Bathrooms are small but of a high standard. An ideal choice for visitors who need to recover from Florence's stressful centre.

～

NEARBY Santissima Annunziata, San Marco, Baptistry, Duomo.
LOCATION in a quiet street, a few minutes' walk N of the Duomo; pay car parking nearby
FOOD breakfast
PRICE ⓔⓔ–ⓔⓔⓔ
ROOMS 4 double, 2 single, 4 family rooms, all with bath or shower, phone, TV, minibar, safe, central heating, air-conditioning, hairdrier
FACILITIES
sitting-room, breakfast-room, bar
CREDIT CARDS AE, DC, EC, MC, V
CHILDREN welcome **DISABLED** no special facilities **PETS** well-behaved dogs accepted
CLOSED never **LANGUAGES** English, French, German
PROPRIETOR Kathleen Doyle Antuono and family

FIRENZE

FLORENCE

RELAIS MARIGNOLLE
~ COUNTRY VILLA ~

Via di San Quirichino a Marignolle 16, 50124 Florence
TEL (055) 2286910 **FAX** (055) 2047396
E-MAIL *relais@marignolle.it*

THE HILLS IMMEDIATELY surrounding Florence are dotted with beautiful properties surrounded by a landscape that belies the fact that only a few kilometres separate them from the chaotic city centre. The Bulleri family have lived in their restored farmhouse set in rambling grounds on a south-facing hillside at Marignolle for some years, but it was only in the summer of 2000 that they opened up their converted outbuildings to guests.

On our visit, sun was pouring in through the picture windows of the large, bright living/breakfast room where comfortable armchairs and sofas, an open fire and an honesty bar encourage one to linger. Bedrooms, while varying in shape and size, are all decorated along the same tasteful lines: stylish country fabrics, padded bed heads, pristine white paintwork and dark parquet floors. The gleaming white bathrooms have large walk-in showers and double basins. Electric kettles (unusual for Italy) and a selection of Antinori wines are supplied in each room. The Bulleris are enthusiastic hosts and will arrange wine tasting tours, golf, shopping trips or even cookery lessons in Signora Bulleri's own kitchen.

~

NEARBY The convent of the Certosa, central Florence (3 km).
LOCATION on a hillside 3 km S of Porta Romana, in own grounds with ample car parking.
FOOD breakfast, light lunch on request
PRICE €€€
ROOMS 9 doubles and twins, all with shower; all rooms have phone, modem port, TV, air-conditioning, mini bar, safe, hair dryer
FACILITIES sitting/breakfast room, gardens, terrace, swimming pool
CREDIT CARDS AE, DC, MC, V
CHILDREN accepted **DISABLED** no special facilities
PETS not accepted **CLOSED** never
LANGUAGES English, French, German **PROPRIETORS** Bulleri family

FIRENZE

FLORENCE

RELAIS DEGLI UFFIZI
~ TOWN GUEST-HOUSE ~

Chiasso de' Baroncelli/Chiasso del Buco, 1650122 Florence
TEL *(055) 2676239* **FAX** *(055) 2657909*
E-MAIL *info@relaisuffiziwebsite www.f* **WEBSITE** *www.relaisuffizi.it*

IT IS EASY TO GET LOST among the warren of narrow passageways that lead off the south side of Piazza Signoria, and there is no helpful sign to guide you to the Relais degli Uffizi. Look out for a pale stone arch that will lead you to its doorway, through which you'll see, adorning the hall, a pretty lunette fresco of a rooftop scene Make straight for the comfortable sitting room, which has a fabulous view over the piazza. A few minutes of watching the comings and goings in this historic square, sizing up the vast outline of the Palazzo Vecchio, and then pondering the extraordinary silhouette of the cathedral dome to the north will immediately give you a flavour of the city.

The ten bedrooms are arranged on two floors and each is very different from the next. All, however, are tastefully decorated and furnished: pastel colours on the walls, a mix of antique and traditional Florentine painted pieces, and original features such as boxed ceilings, creaky parquet floors and even an enormous fireplace that acts as a bed head (this was the kitchen in the original 16thC house). Several rooms have modern four-poster beds draped with filmy white curtains. Bathrooms were being revamped when we visited.

~

NEARBY Ponte Vecchio; Palazzo Vecchio; the Uffizi.
LOCATION in a narrow lane off the south side of Piazza Signoria, with paid car parking nearby
FOOD breakfast
PRICE €€€
ROOMS 10 doubles and twins, 1 single, all with bath or shower; all rooms have phone, TV, air-conditioning, minibar, safe, hairdryer
FACILITIES sitting/breakfast room
CREDIT CARDS AE, DC, MC, V **CHILDREN** accepted **DISABLED** 2 adapted rooms, lift/elevator **PETS** accepted if small **CLOSED** never **LANGUAGES** English, French, Japanese, Spanish, German
PROPRIETOR Elizabetta Matucci

FIRENZE

FLORENCE

RESIDENCE JOHANNA

~ TOWN GUEST-HOUSE ~

Via delle Cinque Giornate 12, 50129 Firenze
TEL & FAX (055) 473377 ·

FLORENCE IS NOTORIOUS for being one of the most expensive cities in Italy for hotel rooms. We were therefore delighted to discover this new 'residence', offering great value for money.

Some way north-west of the centre of the city, but on several bus routes, the Johanna's existence is announced by a discreet brass plaque next to a solid iron gate leading to a pleasant building in its own small gravelled garden.

Inside, you find yourself in an elegant private residence, with cool, cream-coloured walls and high ceilings throughout give pleasant sense of space. At the back of the house, a comfortable sitting-room doubles as reception.

The bedrooms are all fairly large (one particularly so), and are furnished with large beds and a mixture antiques and modern pieces. Tasteful fabrics, predominantly pale green and cream stripes, add style. Bathrooms vary in size, but even the smallest is adequate. Each room has the where-with-all for a simple DIY breakfast: electric kettle, coffee, tea, biscuits and brioche.

~

NEARBY Santa Maria Novella, Fortezza da Basso.
LOCATION in residential area 15 minutes' walk north-west of the station in own garden with limited parking
MEALS breakfast
PRICES doubles €€€€, extra bed €
ROOMS 6 doubles (3 twins), one with bath, the rest with showers; all with TV, 3 with air-conditioning
FACILITIES sitting-room, small garden
SMOKING permitted **CREDIT CARDS** not accepted **CHILDREN** welcome
DISABLED no special facilities but 3 ground-floor bedrooms
PETS accepted **CLOSED** never **LANGUAGES** English, French, German
PROPRIETOR Lea Gulmanelli

FIRENZE

FLORENCE

LE STANZE DI SANTA CROCE
～ TOWN GUEST-HOUSE ～

50122 Florence. Via delle Pinzochere 6
TEL & FAX (055) 2001366
E-MAIL *lestanze@viapinzochere6.it* **WEBSITE** www.viapinzochere6.it

MARIANGELA CATALANI opened her narrow townhouse to guests in 2002. The location couldn't be better for exploring Florence's art treasures, but foodies will also be well pleased with the vicinity of the bustling Sant' Ambrogio food market, plus a glut of good restaurants and wine bars.

The welcoming, informal reception area is on the first floor and leads to a jasmin-scented terrace where breakfast is served in summer or where guests can relax with something cold from the 'honesty fridge.' The same space is cleverly enclosed in colder weather to make a sunny winter garden. The four bedrooms are all very different, but each has been carefully furnished with a mix of old and new. Pale walls contrast with stronger-coloured fabrics on beds and curtains, while traditional beamed ceilings sit well with contemporary, sometimes quirky, light fittings. One room has a curtained four-poster bed; another (at the top of the house) has skylights and a pale acid green and mauve colour scheme. Mariangela cares about her guests' well-being. She serves delicious dinners on request (by candlelight on the terrace) and is full of useful tips on the area.

～

NEARBY Santa Croce; Sant' Ambrogio market; the Duomo.
LOCATION on a side street off Piazza Santa Croce, with paid parking nearby.
FOOD breakfast, dinner on request
PRICE ⓔⓔ
ROOMS 4 doubles and twins, 3 with shower, 1 with own bathroom (including Jacuzzi); all rooms have phone, TV, air- conditioning, hairdryer, safe, modem port
FACILITIES terrace, sitting room
CREDIT CARDS AE, MC, V
CHILDREN accepted
DISABLED not suitable
PETS not accepted
CLOSED never **LANGUAGES** English
PROPRIETOR Mariangela Catalani

FIRENZE

FLORENCE

TORNABUONI BEACCI
∼ TOWN GUEST-HOUSE ∼

Via Tornabuoni 3, 50123 Firenze
TEL (055) 212645, 268377 **FAX** (055) 283594

O NE COULD NOT ASK for more in terms of location. Via Tornabuoni is one of
Florence's most elegant and central shopping streets, where leading
designers such as Gucci, Ferragamo and Ferré have their stores and within easy walking distance are all the main sights of the city. Yet its position
on the fourth and fifth floors in the 15thC Palazzo Minerbetti Strozzi, at
one corner of Piazza Santa Trinita, makes it a haven from Florence's
crowded, noisy streets.

The pensione has a turn-of-the-century atmosphere; fans of E.M.
Forster's A Room With A View will find this a close approximation to the
Edwardian guest-house described in the novel. Many of the rooms have
views, but none so fine as the roof-top terrace, with its plants and pergola,
which looks over the city to the towers and villas of the Bellosguardo hill.
Even in the hot, still days of July and August, you may catch a refreshing
breeze here.

The decoration and furnishings are old-fashioned but well-maintained,
like the house of a maiden aunt. Parquet floors and plain-covered sofas
are much in evidence. Rooms vary – some are quite poky – but new management has been making improvements.

∼

NEARBY Santa Trinita, Ponte Vecchio, Palazzo della Signoria, Uffizi.
LOCATION in centre of town; car parking in private garage nearby (about 20 euros
per day)
FOOD breakfast, dinner, snacks (in summer)
PRICE €€–€€€
ROOMS 8 single, 20 double, all with bath or shower, phone, TV, minibar, air-
conditioning
FACILITIES sitting-room, restaurant, roof-terrace
CREDIT CARDS AE, DC, EC, MC, V **CHILDREN** welcome **DISABLED** difficult
PETS small dogs only **CLOSED** never
LANGUAGES English, French, German, Spanish
PROPRIETOR Francesco Bechi

FIRENZE

FLORENCE

TORRE DI BELLOSGUARDO
∼ COUNTRY VILLA ∼

Via Roti Michelozzi 250124 Firenze
TEL (055) 2298145**FAX** (055) 229008

EVERYBODY HAS HEARD of the hillside of Fiesole, north of Florence, site of the original Etruscan settlement in the area. Less well known, on the southern edge of the city, is the hill of Bellosguardo ('lovely view' in Italian), more discreet in atmosphere and without a busy town to attract trippers. What will draw visitors, however, is this fine hotel – close enough to Florence for easy access but far away enough to guarantee enjoyment of Tuscany's countryside.

As the name suggests, a tower stands at the heart of this 16thC villa, built originally for defence and then surrounded by the trappings of civilization as time passed by. Extraordinary care has been taken to restore the buildings to their former glory after years of abuse as a school in the post-war period. Spacious rooms with painted wood or vaulted ceilings, frescoed walls and the antiques appropriate to the setting create an atmosphere of character and distinction. No two bedrooms are alike and we saw only one that we thought less than admirable. An indoor pool complex incorporating sauna and an underground garage was under construction as we went to press for this edition.

∼

NEARBY Palazzo Pitti, Boboli gardens and other Florence sights.
LOCATION on the hill of Bellosguardo, just S of the city; underground car parking
FOOD breakfast, lunch
PRICE €€€–€€€€; breakfast €;
ROOMS 8 double, 2 single, 6 suites, all with bath; all rooms have phone and central heating; 5 have air-conditioning
FACILITIES sitting-rooms, breakfast-room, bar, garden, indoor swimming-pool
CREDIT CARDS AE, EC, MC, V
CHILDREN welcome
DISABLED no special facilities
PETS accepted **CLOSED** never
LANGUAGES English, German,French
PROPRIETOR Giovanni Franchetti

FIRENZE

FLORENCE

TORRE GUELFA
~ TOWN BED-AND-BREAKFAST ~

Borgo SS Apostoli 8, 50123 Firenze
TEL (055) 2396338 **FAX** (055) 2398577 **E-MAIL** torre.guelfa@flashnet.it
WEBSITE http://home.venere.it/florence/torreguelfa

THERE CAN BE FEW better spots in Florence in which to enjoy a peaceful apperitivo after a hard days' sightseeing: this is the tallest privately-owned tower in the city, dating from the 13thC and enjoying a 360° view over a jumble of rooftops, taking in all the most important landmarks and the countryside beyond.

Until now it has been a short entry in this guide, but we're now featuring it as a full-page, partly because of its populaity, partly because on viewing it again we thought that the Italian-German owners have created such a comfortable and un-stuffy atmosphere rejecting a heavy, Florentine look for a lighter touch.

Bedroom walls are sponge-painted in pastel shades and curtains are mostly fresh, embroidered white cotton. Furniture is a mixture of wrought-iron and prettily-painted pieces, with some antiques. Bathrooms are in smart grey Carrara marble.

One room has its own spacious terrace complete with olive tree: be prepared to fight for it. A glassed-in loggia makes a sunny breakfast room and the double 'salon', with its boxed-wood ceiling and little bar, has a comfortable, relaxing atomosphere.

~

NEARBY Ponte Vecchio, Palazzo Vecchio, Palazzo Pitti.
LOCATION in centre of town in traffic limited area with garage parking nearby
FOOD breakfast
PRICE €€-€€€
ROOMS 1 single, 13 doubles and twins; 2 family rooms, all with bath or shower, phone, TV, air conditioning, minibar
FACILITIES bar, sitting room, breakfast room, terraces
CREDIT CARDS AE, EC, MC, V **CHILDREN** welcome
DISABLED one adapted room
PETS small ones welcome
CLOSED never **LANGUAGES** English, French, German
PROPRIETOR Giancarlo Avuri

FIRENZE

FLORENCE

VILLA AZALEE
~ TOWN HOTEL ~

Viale Fratelli Rosselli 44, 50123 Firenze
TEL (055) 214242 **FAX** (055) 268264

CONVENIENT FOR THE STATION but slightly remote from the monumental district (about 15 minutes by foot) Villa Azalee will appeal to visitors who prefer family-run hotels with some style to larger more luxurious operations. And by the standards of most hotels in Florence, prices are very reasonable. The hotel consists of two buildings: the original 19thC villa and, across the garden, a new annexe, full of the potted azaleas that give the place its name.

A highly individual style has been used in the decoration and furniture: some will find the results delightful, others excessively whimsical. Pastel colours, frilly canopies and matching curtains and bed-covers characterize the bedrooms. They are all air-conditioned, with spotless, new bathrooms. Public rooms are more restrained with an interesting collection of the family's paintings. Breakfast is served either in your room or in the garden (somewhat noisy) or in a separate breakfast-room.

One of the drawbacks of the hotel is its location on the viali (the busy traffic arteries circling Florence). Sound proofing has been used, but rooms in the annexe, or overlooking the garden are best.

~

NEARBY Santa Maria Novella, Ognissanti, San Lorenzo, Duomo.
LOCATION a few minutes' walk W of the main station, towards Porta al Prato; pay car parking nearby (about 15 euros per day)
FOOD breakfast
PRICE €€–€€€
ROOMS 2 single, 22 double, all with bath or shower, air-conditioning, TV, phone, TV, minibar
FACILITIES sitting-room, bar, garden
CREDIT CARDS AE, DC, EC, MC, V **CHILDREN** welcome
DISABLED no special facilities
PETS please check first
CLOSED never **LANGUAGES** English, French
PROPRIETOR Ornella Brizzi

FIRENZE

GIOGOLI

IL MILIONE
~ FARM GUEST-HOUSE ~

Loc. Galluzzo, Via di Giogoli 14, 50124 Firenze
TEL (055) 2048713 **FAX** (055) 2048046

IN MANY WAYS an ideal location for those who like to combine city tourism with a country retreat. Il Milione is theoretically within Florence's city limits, but you could just as well be in deepest Tuscany. Convenient access to the autostrada brings Siena, San Gimignano, Pisa, Lucca and Arezzo all within easy driving distance. Nearby is the famous Certosa di Galluzzo. Yet Il Milione has everything that a farm should have: vines, olives and honey, fresh eggs and vegetables, and acres of countryside to roam in. A swimming-pool and a small lake are added attractions.

The eccentric name originates with Signora Husy's husband (now, alas, dead) Guscelli Brandimarte, a silversmith who, when he wanted to buy the farm, borrowed a million lire from each of his friends, repaying them with examples of his own workmanship. His irrepressible spirit lives on at Il Milione in the sculptures that are scattered throughout the gardens and in the silver place-settings at the dining-table. Rooms and apartments are spread throughout the farm's buildings. Booking ahead is essential. One of the best bargains in the Florence area..

~

NEARBY Florence (8 km); Siena (60 km).
LOCATION 8 km S of city centre, in own grounds; car parking
FOOD self-catering, dinner on request; fresh farm breakfast ingredients supplied
PRICE ⓔ–ⓔⓔ (DB&B)
ROOMS 2 two-person apartments, 5 four-person apartments, all with bath or shower, phone, TV; 3-day minimum stay
FACILITIES sitting-room, dining-room, garden, swimming-pool, bowls, horse-riding
CREDIT CARDS not accepted
CHILDREN welcome
DISABLED no special facilities
PETS not accepted
CLOSED never
LANGUAGES English, German, French
PROPRIETOR Jessica Husy

FIRENZE

GREVE IN CHIANTI

CASTELLO DI UZZANO
∽ COUNTRY APARTMENTS ∽

Via Uzzano 5, Greve in Chianti, 50022 Firenze
TEL (055) 854032 **FAX** (055) 854375

ORIGINALLY A 12THC CASTLE which the additions of centuries have converted to an elegant and civilized country villa, surrounded on its hilltop by stately cypresses and umbrella pines. Adjacent to the villa is a delightful ornamental garden with geometrically laid out box hedges, battered old statues and terracotta urns filled with flowers. On the other side is a formal terrace which is neatly compartmented by gravel paths and weathered stone balustrades.

The apartments surround a courtyard to which the graceful loggia of the castle forms a backdrop. A great deal of imagination and flair has been put into their restoration and decoration. Each has been individually furnished with interesting antiques and fine old prints and paintings of a higher standard than one normally finds in this type of place.

Smart kitchens have been unobtrusively incorporated, but if you prefer to eat out, there are many excellent restaurants in the area.

Undeniably aristocratic, indisputably historical, Castello di Uzzano enables guests to relish an oasis of civilized living.

NEARBY Florence (30 km); Siena (45 km).
LOCATION 1 km N of Greve in own grounds; ample car parking
FOOD none
PRICE €€€€–€€€€€; 3 night minimum stay
ROOMS 6 fully equipped apartments for 2 to 4 persons
FACILITIES gardens, bikes
SMOKING permitted
CREDIT CARDS EC, MC, V
CHILDREN welcome
DISABLED no special facilities
PETS please check first
CLOSED never
LANGUAGES English, French, German
PROPRIETOR Marion de Jacobert

FIRENZE

VILLA DI VIGNAMAGGIO
~ COUNTRY VILLA ~

Greve in Chianti, 50022 Florence
TEL (055) 954661 **FAX** (055) 8544468
E-MAIL agriturismo@vignamaggio.com **WEBSITE** www.vignamaggio.com

CHIANTI HAS MORE THAN ITS SHARE of hill-top villas and castles, now posing as hotels, or, as in this case, self-catering (agriturismo) apartments. Vignamaggio stands out from them all: one of those rare places that made us think twice about advertising it. The villa's first owners were the Gherardini family, of which Mona Lisa, born here in 1479, was a member. This could even have been where she and Leonardo met. More recently, it was the setting for Kenneth Branagh's film of Shakespeare's Much Ado About Nothing.

Villa di Vignamaggio is a warm Tuscan pink. A small formal garden in front gives way to acres of vines. The pool, a short distance from the house, is among fields and trees. The interior is a perfect combination of simplicity and good taste, with the emphasis on natural materials. Beds, chairs and sofas are comfortable and attractive. Old wardrobes cleverly hide small kitchen units. The two public rooms are equally pleasing, and breakfast there or on the terrace is thoughtfully planned, with bread from the local bakery and home-made jam. The staff were charming and helpful when we visited 'Service' is kept to a minimum ("This is not a hotel").

~

NEARBY Greve (5 km); Florence (19 km); Siena (38 km).
LOCATION on its own estate, 5 km SE of Greve on the road to Lamole from the SS222
FOOD breakfast; dinner on three evenings a week
PRICE €€€€–€€€€€
ROOMS 21 rooms, suites, self-catering apartments, for 2-4, all with bath, phone, heating, some air-conditioned
FACILITIES sitting-room, bar, terrace, garden, 2 pools, gym, tennis court, children's playground, walks
CREDIT CARDS AE, EC, MC, V
CHILDREN Children welcome **DISABLED** one apartment **PETS** welcome **CLOSED** never
LANGUAGES English, German, French
PROPRIETOR Gianni Nunziante

FIRENZE

MONTEFIRIDOLFI

IL BORGHETTO
~ COUNTRY VILLA ~

Via Collina S Angelo 23, Montefiridolfi, S. Casciano Val di Pesa, 50020 Firenze
TEL (055) 8244442 **FAX** (055) 8244247

DISCRETION, TASTE AND REFINEMENT are the key characteristics of this family guest-house, only recently opened but already appreciated by a discerning (and returning) clientèle that enjoys civilized living in a peaceful, bucolic setting.

A manicured gravel drive, leads past the lawn, with its rose beds and cypress trees, to the main buildings, which include the remains of two 15thC military towers. From a covered terrace, where breakfast is accompanied by views of miles of open countryside, a broad-arched entrance leads to the open-plan ground floor of the main villa. Within, the usual starkness of the Tuscan style has been softened by the use of muted tones in the wall colours and fabrics. Comfortable furniture abounds without cluttering the spacious, airy quality of the public areas. Upstairs, in the bedrooms (some of which are not particularly large), floral wallpaper and subdued lighting create a balmy, relaxed atmosphere. No intrusive phone calls or blaring televisions; a mini-bar would be considered vulgar.

Even the refined like a swim; but for those who consider swimming-pools raucous, there is a soothing water garden.

~

NEARBY Florence (18 km); Siena (45 km); San Gimignano (40 km).
LOCATION hillside villa in its own grounds; ample car parking
FOOD breakfast; lunch and dinner if sufficient numbers request
PRICE €€€; 2-day min. stay
ROOMS 6 doubles, 2 suites all with shower
FACILITIES sitting-room, dining-room, terrace, gardens, swimming-pool, cookery courses
CREDIT CARDS EC, MC, V
CHILDREN not suitable for very young children
DISABLED one suitable room with bathroom
PETS not accepted **CLOSED** Nov to Mar
LANGUAGES English, French, German
PROPRIETOR Antonio Cavallini

FIRENZE

MERCATALE VAL DI PESA

SALVADONICA
COUNTRY GUEST-HOUSE

Via Grevigiana 82, 50024 Mercatale Val di Pesa (Firenze)
TEL (055) 8218039 **FAX** (055) 8218043
E-MAIL salvadonica@tin.it **WEBSITE** www.cosmos.it/salvadonica

TWO ENTERPRISING SISTERS have turned their family's 14thC farm properties into a thriving guest-house and apartment complex, in rolling countryside, south of Florence, a conversion carried out with style and panache, exploiting the buildings' character and position to the maximum. The central house is a warm pink and is surrounded by stone farmhouses with their details picked out in brick. In the paved courtyard stands a single umbrella pine. The enthusiasm of Francesca and Beatrice and their friendly welcome makes for a vivacious, friendly atmosphere.

Elegance and comfort characterize the rooms and apartments, with individual variations on the classic rustic ingredients of beamed ceilings, simple white plaster walls and warm, terracotta-tiled floors. A particularly impressive apartment with refined brick vaulting and columns looks more like the crypt of a Renaissance church than a converted cow byre. With a swimming-pool, tennis-court and riding (nearby) as well as easy access to Tuscany's most important art cities, your stay at Salvadonica will seem all too short. A recent visitor was thoroughly enchanted.

NEARBY Florence (18 km); Siena (40 km).
LOCATION 18 km S of Florence, leaving Siena highway (SS2) at San Casciano Val di Pesa; own grounds, car parking
FOOD breakfast, snacks
PRICE €€€
ROOMS 5 double, all with bath or shower, phone; 10 apartments for two to four persons
FACILITIES Facilities breakfast-room, garden, swimming-pool, billiards, tennis, play area
CREDIT CARDS AE, DC, EC, MC, V **CHILDREN** welcome
DISABLED two adapted rooms
PETS not accepted **CLOSED** Nov to Feb **LANGUAGES** English, German
PROPRIETORS Beatrice and Francesca Baccetti

FIRENZE

PANZANO IN CHIANTI

VILLA LE BARONE
~ COUNTRY VILLA ~

Via San Leolino 19, Panzano in Chianti,, 50020 Firenze
TEL (055) 852621 **FAX** (055) 852277

ONE OF THE GREAT DELIGHTS of aristocrats finding their villas too large and expensive to run is that, when they retire to the tastefully converted chicken-house, they leave behind them family collections of antiques, paintings and objets d'art, painstakingly put together over the centuries, which no interior decorator could hope to imitate. Such is the case with Le Barone, a small gem of a villa, which still retains the atmosphere of a private house rather than a hotel.

An air of unforced refinement and aristocratic ease in a setting of withdrawn tranquillity will immediately strike any visitor. The public rooms are small in scale and slightly cluttered; in the sitting-room, with its blue and yellow sofas, dominated at one end by a carved-stone fireplace, there is a collection of family paintings and of books which you are welcome to read. Just outside, is a long gravel terrace, for breakfast in fine weather or drinks in the evening. The bar, where you help yourself and write it down in a book, has seats made from wine-barrels and a cradle full of flowers. Bedrooms, particularly those in the main villa (reached by a spiral staircase), are tastefully furnished.

~

NEARBY Greve (6 km); Florence (29 km); Siena (33 km).
LOCATION 6 km S of Greve in Chianti in its own grounds; ample car parking
FOOD breakfast, lunch, dinner, snacks
PRICE €€€ (DB&B)(min 3 nights)
ROOMS 25 double, all with bath or shower; phone; 5 with air-conditioning
FACILITIES Facilities sitting-rooms, breakfast-room, restaurant, bar, swimming-pool, tennis
CREDIT CARDS AE, MC, V
CHILDREN welcome
DISABLED not suitable
PETS dogs not allowed
CLOSED Nov to Mar
LANGUAGES English **PROPRIETOR** Duchessa Franca di Grazzano Visconti

FIRENZE

PANZANO IN CHIANTI

VILLA ROSA
~ COUNTRY GUEST-HOUSE ~

Via S. Leolino 59, Panzano in Chianti (Firenze)
TEL (055) 852577 **FAX** (055) 8560835 **E-MAIL** torre.guelfa@flashnet.it
WEBSITE http://home.venere.it/florence/torreguelfa

A RECENT ADDITION to the countless hotels and guest houses in this part of Chianti, Villa Rosa is a solid structure dating from the early 1900s. Looming over the road from Panzano to Radda, its appearance makes a refreshing change form the usual rustic stone Tuscan farmhouse formula: it is painted bright pink.

Inside, a light touch is evident in the the decoration. The terracotta floors and white walls downstairs are typical, but bedrooms have pastel-coloured, sponged paintwork, wrought-iron four poster beds and a mixture of wicker furniture, toether with antique pieces here and there. The attractive, rather quirky, light fittings are by a local craftsman. Bathrooms also have touches of colour while heated towel rails add a hint of luxury.

The building is too near the road to be ideally situated, but at the back there is a peaceful, partially shaded terrace for outdoor eating while the garden slopes up the hillside to a pleasant pool and open, vine-striped countryside. Reasonable prices and a relaxed style of management should make this hotel very popular. We look forward to readers' reports.

~

NEARBY Florence (35km); Siena (35km).
LOCATION 3 km SE of Panzano on Radda road in own grounds with private car parking
FOOD breakfast, dinner
PRICE €€€€; dinner€ without wine
ROOMS 12 doubles and twins, all with bath or shower, phone, TV, minibar
FACILITIES garden, terraces, sitting room, restaurant, pool
SMOKING allowed
CREDIT CARDS AE, EC, MC, V **CHILDREN** welcome
DISABLED one room at street level with adapted bathroom
PETS accepted
CLOSED mid Nov-before Easter
LANGUAGES English, French, German
PROPRIETOR Sabine Buntenbach

FIRENZE

PANZANO IN CHIANTI

VILLA SANGIOVESE
～ COUNTRY VILLA ～

Piazza Bucciarelli 5, 50020 Panzano in Chianti, Firenze
TEL (055) 852461 **FAX** (055) 852463
WEBSITE www.italyone.com/villasangiovese

THE BLEULERS ONCE MANAGED the Tenuta di Ricavo at Castellina (page 85). It's now more than ten years since they started this new venture in Panzano, a few miles to the north. Readers' reports are consistently appreciative.

The main villa is a neat stone-and-stucco house fronting directly on to a back-street; potted plants and a brass plate beside the doorway are the only signs of a hotel. Attached to this house is an old rambling stone building beside a flowery, gravelled courtyard-terrace offering splendid views. The landscaped garden below includes a fair-sized pool. Inside, all is mellow, welcoming and stylish, with carefully chosen antique furnishings against plain, pale walls. Bedrooms, some with wood-beamed ceilings are spacious, comfortably, and tastefully restrained in decoration. The dining-room is equally simple and stylish, with subdued wall lighting and bent-wood chairs on a tiled floor.

A limited but interestng á la carte menu is offered, which changes each night – service on the terrace in summer. A recent reporter praised the food and the wine.

～

NEARBY Greve (5 km); Siena (30 km); Florence (30 km).
LOCATION on edge of town, 5 km S of Greve; with large garden and ample car parking
FOOD Meals breakfast, lunch, dinner
PRICE rooms €€; suites €€€€; meals from €
ROOMS 16 double, 1 single, 2 suites, all with bath or shower; all rooms have phone, TV on request
FACILITIES dining-room, 2 sitting-rooms, library, bar, terrace, swimming-pool
CREDIT CARDS MC, V **CHILDREN** accepted
DISABLED no special facilities
PETS not accepted
CLOSED Christmas to Feb; restaurant only, Wed
MANAGERS Ulderico and Anna Maria Bleuler

FIRENZE

REGGELLO

VILLA RIGACCI
~ HILLTOP VILLA ~

Loc. Vággio 76, Regello 50066, Florence
TEL (055) 865 6718 **FAX** (055) 865 6537
E-MAIL hotel@villarigacci.it

THIS CREEPER-COVERED 15thC farmhouse stands in a beautiful secluded spot – a hill-top surrounded by olive groves, pines, chestnut trees and meadows – yet only a few kilometres from the Florence-Rome autostrada and a short drive from Florence and Arezzo.

The house achieves a cosy and relaxed atmosphere in spite of its four-star facilities. It is furnished as a cherished family home, much of it reflecting Signor Pierazzi's Camargue background, including some lovely antiques from the region and prints of Camargue horses. Bedrooms – the best are gloriously spacious and full of gleaming antiques – overlook the gardens and tranquil swimming-pool.

The sitting-room has an open fire in chilly weather; the breakfast-room is a converted stable with the hay racks still on the walls. The elegantly rustic dining-room offers local, Italian and French-influenced dishes. Guests are well cared for – if you are peckish, for example, you can order snacks or light meals at any time of the day. In summer, fish and meat are cooked al fresco on the large outdoor barbecue. Next to the house is a tiny family chapel where Mass is still occasionally said.

~

NEARBY Florence (35 km); Arezzo (45 km).
LOCATION 300 m N of Vággio, 30 km SE of Florence; exit Incisa from A1; with car parking and shady, tree-filled gardens
FOOD breakfast, lunch, dinner
PRICE €€€
ROOMS 3 single, 15 double,
4 suites; all with bath and shower, TV, minibar, air-conditioning, heating, phone
FACILITIES sitting-room, restaurant, bar, terrace, garden, pool
CREDIT CARDS AE, DC, EC, MC, V **CHILDREN** welcome
DISABLED no special facilities **PETS** accepted **CLOSED** never
LANGUAGES English, German, French, Spanish, Arabic
PROPRIETORS Federico Pierazzi

FIRENZE

SESTO FIORENTINO

VILLA VILLORESI
~ TOWN VILLA ~

Via Campi 2, Colonnata di Sesto Fiorentino, 50019 Firenze
TEL (055) 443212 **FAX** (055) 442063
E-MAIL cvillor@tin.it

THE ARISTOCRATIC VILLA VILLORESI looks rather out of place in what is now an industrial suburb of Florence, but once in the house and gardens you suddenly feel a million miles away from modern, bustling Florence. Contessa Cristina Villoresi is a warm hostess who has captured the hearts of many transatlantic and other guests. It is thanks to her that the villa still has the feel of a private home – all rather grand, if a little faded and standing still in time.

As you make your way through the building, each room seems to have some curiosity or feature of the past. The entrance hall is a superb gallery of massive chandeliers, frescoed walls, antiques and lofty potted plants. Then there is the first-floor loggia, the longest in Tuscany, on to which five of the finest bedrooms open. Another, on the ground floor, has crystal chandeliers, floor-to-ceiling frescoes, and a canopied bed. Other bedrooms, however, are very different: small and plain with simple painted furniture, and looking on to an inner courtyard.

In the two dining-rooms Tuscan specialities are served. Contessa Villoresi runs residential courses on the Italian Renaissance.

~

NEARBY Florence (8 km).
LOCATION 9 km NW of Florence; adequate parking
FOOD breakfast, lunch, dinner
PRICE €–€€€; DB&B €€€ with breakfast; meals €€; 10% reductions Nov-Dec, Jan-Mar and Aug, and for children
ROOMS 23 double, 5 single; all with bath, shower, TV on request, heating, phone
FACILITIES sitting-rooms, res-taurant, bar, terraces, garden, pool, walks
CREDIT CARDS AE, DC, MC, V **CHILDREN** welcome
DISABLED ground floor rooms
PETS not in public rooms
CLOSED never
LANGUAGES English, German, French
PROPRIETOR Contessa Cristina Villoresi

FIRENZE

TRESPIANO

VILLA LE RONDINI
~ VILLA HOTEL ~

Via Bolognese Vecchia 224, Trespiano, 50139 Firenze
TEL (055) 400081 **FAX** (055) 268212

THE SWALLOWS that give the hotel its name can be seen in the evening, skimming over one of the most pleasant swimming-pools in the Florence area, set in shady olive groves and with a view over the city second to none. One of the most attractive features of Villa Le Rondini is its enviable location: only seven kilometres from Florence's crowded centre (reachable by bus) yet in the middle of acres of parkland on top of Monte Rinaldi, north of the city. The grounds are a delight to wander through.

The long, ochre-coloured, 16thC villa is surrounded by lawns and terraces, and contains the principal public rooms and the main bedrooms (the remainder are in two other more modern buildings nearby). The furnishings are a not completely successful eclectic mixture of rustic antiques and outdated hotel furniture. The sitting-room is full of comfortable couches and chairs, dominated at one end by an immense, carved stone fireplace.

Bedrooms vary in size and furnishings, some with wrought-iron beds and antiques, others more modern in style; the suites have the best views. All have decent bathrooms.

~

NEARBY Florence (7 km); Mugello valley.
LOCATION 7 km north of Florence on the old road to Bologna, in own grounds; plenty of parking
FOOD Meals breakfast, lunch, dinner
PRICE €€€–€€€€
ROOMS 43 double, all with bath or shower, phone, TV, minibar, air-conditioning
FACILITIES sitting-rooms, restaurant, conference room, park, swimming-pool with bar, tennis, riding, heliport
CREDIT CARDS AE, DC, EC, MC, V **CHILDREN** welcome
DISABLED some suitable rooms
PETS please check first **CLOSED** never
LANGUAGES English, French, German
PROPRIETOR Francesca Reali

FIRENZE

VILLA CAMPESTRI
~ COUNTRY HOTEL ~

Via di Campestri 19/22, Vicchio di Mugello, 50039 Firenze
TEL (055) 8490107 **FAX** (055) 8490108

MUGELLO IS THE NAME of the little-visited area north-east of Florence characterized by dramatic mountain landscapes bordering wide river valleys. Wilder than Chianti, it is increasingly frequented by Florentines in search of unspoilt countryside without the bill-boards that are becoming eyesores in the more popular parts of Tuscany. Unfortunately, you will not find too many decent hotels either, and Villa Campestri is by far the most stylish in the area.

The Renaissance villa, a square, imposing building in off-white stucco, stands on top of a hill in open countryside. Before being turned into a hotel it was owned by the same family for over six hundred years. Much of its former grandeur remains: on the ground floor, stately public rooms paved in stone or dark terracotta are hung with faded tapestries and oil paintings. One of them has fine stained windows executed by Chini in Liberty style. The restaurant is one of the best in the area. It is also a popular place for wedding parties, which can be a nuisance at weekends.) Bedrooms are equally grand in the villa, though a few more homely ones have been added in the next-door farmhouse.

~

NEARBY Florence (35 km).
LOCATION 3 km S of Vicchio, in own grounds; ample car parking
FOOD breakfast, dinner, snacks
PRICE €€€-€€€€
ROOMS 14 double, 6 suites, 1 single, all with bath or shower, phone, satellite TV, minibar
FACILITIES sitting-rooms, restaurant, bar, swimming-pool, horse-riding; golf nearby
CREDIT CARDS EC, MC, V **CHILDREN** welcome
DISABLED 4 adapted rooms
PETS small dogs, only on request
CLOSED Jan to Mar **LANGUAGES** English
PROPRIETOR Paolo Pasquali

GROSSETO

PORTO ERCOLE

IL PELLICANO
~ SEASIDE HOTEL ~

Cala dei Santi, 58018 Porto Ercole Grosseto
TEL (0564) 858111 **FAX** (0564) 833418
E-MAIL Pr@Pellicanohotel.com **WEBSITE** www.Pellicanohotel.com

PORTO ERCOLE IS ONE of those fashionable little harbours where wealthy Romans moor their boats at weekends. Il Pellicano is an elegant, russet-coloured vine-clad villa with gardens tumbling down to the rocky shoreline, where the flat rocks have been designated the hotel's 'private beach'. It offers the luxury and exclusivity you might expect from a very expensive four-star seaside hotel but manages at the same time to preserve the style and informality of a private Tuscan villa – and the exposed beams, stone arches and antique features make it feel much older than it really is. Antique country-house furnishings are offset by whitewashed walls, brightly coloured stylish sofas and large vases of flowers. Fish and seafood are the best things in the restaurant – if you can stomach the prices. Meals in summer are served on the delightful open-air terrace in the garden, or beside the pool where the spread of antipasti is a feast for the eyes. Service is impeccable. Peaceful bedrooms, many in two-storey cottages, combine antiques and modern fabrics. The majority are cool and spacious, and all of them have a terrace or balcony. Watch out for swarms of mosquitoes, warns our inspector.

NEARBY Orbetello (16 km).
LOCATION 4 km from middle of resort; car parking
FOOD breakfast, lunch, dinner
PRICE €€€€
ROOMS 27 double; 14 suites (6 de luxe), all with bath and shower; all rooms have central heating, air-conditioning, minibar, phone, cable TV
FACILITIES restaurants, bars, sitting area; terraces; beauty centre, heated sea water swimming-pool; clay-pigeon shooting, tennis, riding, water-skiing
CREDIT CARDS AE, DC, EC, MC, V **CHILDREN** accepted over 12
DISABLED access difficult but some ground floor rooms
PETS not accepted **CLOSED** Closed Nov to Mar
LANGUAGES English, French, Spanish, German **MANAGER** Mrs Cinzia Fanciulli

LUCCA

LUCCA

LOCANDA ELISA
~ COUNTRY VILLA ~

Via Nuova per Pisa (SS 12 bis), Massa Pisana, 55050 Lucca
TEL (0583) 379737 **FAX** (0583) 379019

A FRENCH OFFICIAL of the Napoleonic times who accompanied the Emperor's sister, Elisa Baciocchi, to Lucca acquired this 18thC villa for his own residence. Perhaps that accounts for the discernibly French style of the house that makes it unique among Tuscan hotels. A square building, three storeys high, painted in an arresting blue with windows and cornices picked out in gleaming white, the villa stands just off the busy old Pisa-Lucca road.

The restorers have fortunately avoided the oppressive Empire style (which, in any case, the small rooms would not have borne) and aimed throughout at lightness and delicacy. The entrance is a symphony in wood, with geometrically patterned parquet flooring and panelled walls, and the illusion of space created with large mirrors. To the right is a small sitting-room, furnished with fine antiques and Knole sofas. A round 19thC conservatory is now the restaurant. Each suite has been individually decorated using striped, floral and small-check patterns and yet more antiques – no expense has been spared. Sister hotel of the Principessa across the road, the Elisa is a notable step up in taste and refinement.

~

NEARBY Lucca (3 km); Pisa (15 km).
LOCATION 3 km S of Lucca on the old road to Pisa, in its own grounds; car parking
FOOD breakfast, lunch, dinner
PRICE €€€–€€€€
ROOMS 1 double, 1 single, 8 suites, all with bath or shower, phone, TV, air-conditioning
FACILITIES sitting-rooms, garden, swimming-pool
CREDIT CARDS AE, DC, EC, MC, V
CHILDREN welcome but 3rd beds are not possible
DISABLED some ground floor rooms but no special bathrooms
PETS small dogs (surcharge)
CLOSED early Jan to early Feb **LANGUAGES** English, German
PROPRIEOTR Alessandra Delgrande

LUCCA

PIETRASANTA

ALBERGO PIETRASANTA
~ TOWN HOTEL ~

Via Garibaldi 35, 55045 Pietrasanta, Lucca
TEL (0584) 793726 **FAX** (0584) 793726 **E-MAIL** E mail a.pietrasanta
@versilia.toscana.it **WEBSITE** www.albergopietrasanta.com

PIETRASANTA (THE 'SAINTED STONE') has long been associated with the
marble industry. The world-famous quarries at Carrara are nearby, and
the attractive little town thrives on marble studios, bronze foundries and a
sub-culture of artists from all over the world. Recently, tourism here has
moved up-market, and the Pietrasanta is a response to this development.
Opened in 1997, the hotel occupies elegant 17thC Palazzo Barsanti-
Bonetti. The interior maintains many of the embellishments of a noble-
man's house: intricate plasterwork, delicate frescoes, a couple of superbly
carved marble fireplaces, spacious rooms and antiques. However, the
addition of the owners' contemporary art collection adds a totally new
dimension.

The comfortable, un-fussy bedrooms have warm, parquet floors, armchairs, smart fabrics and varying colour schemes. Thoughtful extras (cool
linen sheets, plenty of mirrors, well-designed lighting and the tray of vin
santo and biscuits) impressed our inspector. Downstairs, the winter garden doubles as breakfast room and bar while the pretty gravelled garden,
dominated by three old palm trees, is a cool spot in summer.

~

NEARBY Pisa (25 km); Lucca (25 km); beaches (4 km).
LOCATION in town centre on pedestrian street; private garage (¡ per day)
FOOD breakfast
PRICE €€€–€€€€
ROOMS 1 single, 8 doubles, 10 suites, all with a bath or shower, TV, phone,
minibar, air-conditioning, safe
FACILITIES winter garden, gym, Turkish bath, garden
CREDIT CARDS AE, DC, EC, MC, V **CHILDREN** welcome
DISABLED 2 adapted rooms **PETS** on request **CLOSED** 6 Jan-28 Feb
LANGUAGES English, French, German
PROPRIETOR Marisa Giuliano

LUCCA

SANTA MARIA DEL GIUDICE

VILLA RINASCIMENTO
~ COUNTRY VILLA ~

Loc. Santa Maria del Giudice, 55058 Lucca
TEL (0583) 378292 **Fax** (0583) 370238

ALMOST EXACTLY HALF-WAY between Pisa and Lucca, this hillside villa presents, at first sight, something of an architectural conundrum. On the right-hand side is a rosy coloured, rustic Renaissance villa, three storeys high, constructed with a mixture of brick and stone. Its main feature is a lovely corner loggia, enclosed by four brick arches supported by Doric columns in stone. On the left, it is joined by a much simpler farmhouse structure. The two are united by a long, paved terrace with lemon trees in large terracotta pots. One can breakfast here or take an aperitivo in the evening.

Inside, a more uniform rustic style prevails. The public rooms are all in a row, facing the terrace, and distinguished by having either exposed-beam or brick-vaulted ceilings, all immaculately restored and including interesting features such as the remnants of an old stone olive-press. Great effort has been put into the bedroom furnishings. Some of the bathrooms are small, but adequate.

Up the hill from the villa is the annex, with some more modern rooms and studios, and a pool designed to exploit to the full its hillside position.

~

NEARBY Lucca (9 km); Pisa (11 km).
LOCATION 9 km SW of Lucca in its own grounds; ample car parking
FOOD breakfast, dinner
PRICE €-€€
ROOMS 17 double, all with bath or shower, phone; some with TV; 4 simpler rooms and 6 studios (one-week rents from Saturdays) in annexe
FACILITIES sitting-rooms, bar, restaurant, swimming-pool
CREDIT CARDS EC, MC, V **CHILDREN** welcome
DISABLED one room with bathroom
PETS please check first **CLOSED** Nov to Mar; restaurant only, Wed
LANGUAGES English, German, French, Dutch
PROPRIETOR Carla Zaffora

PISA

MONTECATINI VAL DI CECINA

IL FRASSINELLO
~ FARMHOUSE ~

Montecatini Val di Cecina, 56040 Pisa
TEL (0588) 30080 **FAX** (0588) 30080

THE DIFFICULT UNSURFACED ROAD that brings you from Montecatini to Il Frassinello seems to last for ever and is certainly not for the weak-spirited. But it is also a guarantee of seclusion. You arrive at your destination to be greeted by the redoubtable Signora Schlubach, who decided to retire here and "not see too much action".

If ever a place has received the imprint of its owner, this is it. The spacious, pleasantly proportioned interiors are filled with the results of a lifetime's collecting on various continents: zebra rugs on the floors, the mounted heads of at least four different types of antelope, a bronze angel hovering over the kitchen door.

There are three rooms in the main villa, and four large self-contained apartments with new bathrooms in a separate building, each with a little kitchen and their own entrance and private terrace, where the minimum stay is three nights.

Guests are not expected to do very much: just relax, take a stroll down to the deer farm, or read a book. Breakfast is taken either in the homely kitchen, or outside under the wisteria-covered pergola.

~

NEARBY Volterra (23 km).
LOCATION 5 km from Montecatini Val di Cecina in middle of countryside
FOOD Meals breakfast; dinner on request (sometimes)
PRICE rooms €); apartment €)€)€)€) per week; discounts for longer stays
ROOMS 4 double all with bath or shower; 4 apartments
FACILITIES sitting-room, garden
CREDIT CARDS not accepted
CHILDREN welcome
DISABLED not suitable
PETS small dogs**CLOSED** Oct to Easter
LANGUAGES English, French, German, Spanish
PROPRIETOR Elga Schlubach

PISA

PUGNANO

CASETTA DELLE SELVE
~ COUNTRY BED-AND-BREAKFAST ~

56010 Pugnano, Pisa
TEL & FAX (050) 850359 *56010 Pugnano, Pisa*

YET ANOTHER elevated Tuscan farmhouse, but this one has a personality all of its own thanks to the owner, Nicla Menchi, a most unusual host. The approach to the white building is through a thick chestnut wood. Once at the top of the rough 2-km drive, the peaceful surroundings, the flower-filled garden and the wonderful views from the red-tiled terrace start to work their magic.

The interiors are very different from the norm. For a start, Nicla's own vivid paintings occupy much of the wall space. The house is exceptionally well-maintained and the bedrooms have bold, bright colour schemes involving bedheads, rugs, bedspreads (all handmade by Nicla) and, of course, her pictures. It might be a little fussy for some tastes; even the coat hangers are colour co-ordinated. However, public areas are a little more restrained, but still full of pictures, books and ornaments. Breakfast (including fresh eggs, home-made cakes and jams) is, when possible, served on the terrace.

Nicla Menchi's enthusiasm for her home and her guests is infectious and many leave as her friend.

~

NEARBY Lucca (10km); Pisa (12 km); Beaches (15 km).
LOCATION In countryside 2 km off SS12, E of Pugnano, 10 km SW of Lucca; private car parking
FOOD breakfast
PRICE €€; minimum 3-day stay
ROOMS 6 doubles, all with bath or shower (two are adjacent)
FACILITIES garden, terrace, sitting-room
CREDIT CARDS not accepted
CHILDREN Children 12 years and up
DISABLED not suitable
PETS accepted **CLOSED** never
LANGUAGES French, a little English **PROPRIETOR** Nicla Menchi

PISTOIA

MASSA E COZZILE

VILLA PASQUINI
~ COUNTRY VILLA ~

Via Vacchereccia 56, Margine Coperta, Massa e Cozzile, 51010 Pistoia
TEL (0572) 72205 **FAX** (0572)910888

STAY AT VILLA PASQUINI and you step back into the 19thC. Little has changed here, either in furnishings, or decoration, since then. Until five years ago, it was the autumn retreat of an aristocratic Roman family, the Pasquinis; then it was bought, fully furnished, by the present incumbents, who have lovingly preserved it, combining a family home with a most unusual hotel. Though it is something of a museum piece, the atmosphere is not stuffy. The family's enthusiasm is infectious, and the welcome warm.

The bedrooms are, of course, all different, some quite grand (but not intimidating) with canopied beds. Bathrooms are old-fashioned, but well equipped. Many boast wonderful trompe l'oeil frescoes – lie in your tub contemplating a lakeland scene with swans and distant mountains.

In the attractive dining-room – originally the entrance hall – the emphasis is on traditional recipes. Our reporter chose the fixed-price menu, was served five delicious courses and thought the price reasonable.

Outside, the gardens and terraces are lush with flowers.

~

NEARBY Montecatini Terme (8 km); Lucca (40 km); Pisa (60 km).
LOCATION off minor road 6 km N of Montecatini Terme in own grounds; ample car parking
FOOD breakfast, dinner
PRICE doubles €
ROOMS 12 double, all with bath and shower, central heating
FACILITIES 2 sitting-rooms, dining-room, terraces, garden, walks
CREDIT CARDS AE, EC, MC, V
CHILDREN welcome
DISABLED some suitable rooms
PETS not accepted
CLOSED 30 Nov to 15 Mar
LANGUAGES English, German, French
PROPRIETORS Innocenti family

PISTOIA

MONTEVETTOLINI

VILLA LUCIA

~ FARMHOUSE BED-AND-BREAKFAST ~

Via dei Bronzoli 144, Montevettolini, 51010 Pistoia
TEL (0572) 617790 **FAX** (0572) 628817
E-MAIL villalucia@yahoo.com **WEBSITE** www.boftuscany.com

LUCIA VALLERA also calls her delightful hillside farmhouse the 'B & B of Tuscany' and runs her establishment along English bed-and-breakfast lines – guests and family mingle informally, eating together in the traditional Tuscan kitchen or at the huge wooden table in the dining-room if numbers require.

A strong Californian influence can be felt in the cooking and in the laid-back, elegant style of the place. (Lucia is an American of Italian extraction who has recently returned to Italy after living in the States.) There are plenty of up-to-date touches: CD player, satellite TV, computer. The clientèle, too, is mainly American – lawyers, doctors and so on – often on return visits.

The dining-room has various dressers crammed with colourful china and glass; there is a double sitting-room with comfortable sofas and armchairs in traditional fabrics, plus shelves of books. Bedrooms are attractive, with working fireplaces, patchwork bedspreads, terracotta floors and antique furniture. Bathrooms are decked in blue and white tiles, and spotless. The house has a lovely garden, and looks up to the old town of Montevettolini.

~

NEARBY Montecatini Terme, Lucca, Vinci.
LOCATION on hillside outside Montevettolini, in own grounds, with ample car parking
FOOD breakfast; dinner on request
PRICE €€€–€€€€
ROOMS 5 double, 2 apartments for 2; all with bath and shower, either adjoining or across the hall, all with heating
FACILITIES sitting-room, conference room, terraces, garden, small pool
CREDIT CARDS none **CHILDREN** welcome **DISABLED** no special facilities
PETS not accepted **CLOSED** Nov to Apr **LANGUAGES** English, French, Spanish, German
PROPRIETOR Lucia Vallera

PISTOIA

PISTOIA

VILLA VANNINI
~ COUNTRY VILLA ~

Villa di Piteccio, 51030 Pistoia
TEL (0573) 42031 **FAX** (0573) 26331

HERE IS A REAL GEM, well off the beaten track, and a complete contrast to
the usual Tuscan villa. It has an Alpine feel: fir trees all around; low
ceilings; green shutters; a little Swiss-style clock tower – and miles of
marked footpaths all around, eventually leading up to the ski resort of
Abetone. It is a haven for serious walkers.

The atmosphere at Villa Vannini is that of a private country house:
there are no hotel signs. You will be greeted by an over-enthusiastic dog.
An inviting smell of wood smoke pervades. The food served in the charming dining-room or on the terrace under huge white umbrellas is carefully
prepared and elegantly presented. Breakfasts are 'excellent' too, according to a recent reporter. Bedrooms are well above the standard for the
price, beautifully and individually furnished, with polished parquet floors,
oriental rugs, brass or wood bedsteads and lovely antique furniture and
mirrors. Although Signora Vannini, is about the place less than she was –
she now has help from a delightful couple, the Borderones, whose cooking
is 'inspirational and exquisitely fresh' – you'll still get a warm welcome.
We've had an exceptional number of warmly approving readers' letters
about the place since the last edition.

~

NEARBY Pistoia, Florence (25 km); Lucca (25 km); Pistoiese hills.
LOCATION 6 km N of Pistoia on hillside, in private garden, with car parking
FOOD Meals breakfast, lunch, dinner
PRICE doubles €€€ (reductions for minimum of 3 days' stay); dinner €
without wine
ROOMS 8 double with bath and central heating
FACILITIES 2 sitting-rooms, games room, dining-room, terrace
CREDIT CARDS EC, MC, V **CHILDREN** not suitable
DISABLED no special facilities
PETS not accepted **CLOSED** never
LANGUAGES English, German, French **PROPRIETOR** Maria-Rosa Vannini

PRATO

BACCHERETO

FATTORIA DI BACCHERETO
~ COUNTRY GUEST-HOUSE ~

Loc. Bacchereto, Via Fontemorana 179, 50042 Prato
TEL (055) 8717191 **FAX** (055) 8717191

ONE OF THE MOST ATTRACTIVE aspects of Fattoria di Bacchereto is its location high in the steep foothills of the Appenines, part of the famous Carmignano wine-growing district (which produces Italy's oldest recognized wine). Entirely isolated, with panoramic views, this little-frequented part of Tuscany is perfect for those who like to combine some city tourism (Florence, Pistoia, Lucca and Pisa are all within driving distance) with country walks and rural peace.

But do not expect luxury: the Fattoria is a working farm and the accommodation is relatively simple. The bedrooms and apartments are spread across the main villa, a rambling 18thC building with terraces and an arched loggia, and simpler farmhouses nearby. The rooms are furnished with time-worn rustic antiques, some in need of restoration, in a setting of terracotta floors and exposed-beam ceilings. The bathrooms are basic but functional.

Outside the villa are pergolas and an ornamental garden with a pond and a fountain, and slightly down the hillside is a small swimming-pool. Breakfast is eaten at a long table near the kitchen; for other meals there is the excellent family restaurant nearby.
~

NEARBY Florence (25 km); Pistoia (18 km).
LOCATION 20 km W of Florence, near Carmignano, in own grounds; car parking
FOOD breakfast
PRICE €
ROOMS 7 double, some with private bathrooms; 3 apartments for 4 to 6 persons
FACILITIES breakfast-room, sitting-room, gardens, swimming-pool; family restaurant nearby
CREDIT CARDS not accepted **CHILDREN** welcome
DISABLED not suitable
PETS on request **CLOSED** never
LANGUAGES English, French
PROPRIETOR Rossella Bencini Tesi

PRATO

PRATO

VILLA RUCELLAI
~ COUNTRY VILLA ~

Via di Canneto 16, Prato, 50047 Firenze
TEL & FAX (0574) 460392
E-MAIL canneto@scotty.masternet.it **WEBSITE** www.itwg.com/itw11448.asp

INDUSTRIAL PRATO creeps almost to the door of this mellow old villa, and a railway line skirts the property, but this should not deter you from staying in this special place. The views from the loggia and lovely terrace – filled with lemon trees – are unsightly, but are more than compensated for by the cultured atmosphere of the house, the warm welcome and the modest prices. Behind the estate rise the beautiful Pratese hills, which can be explored on foot.

The origins of the Villa Rucellai date back to a medieval watchtower, and it has been in the venerable Rucellai family since 1740. Guests have the run of the main part of the house, with its baronial hall and comfortable, lived-in sitting-room, filled with pictures and books. Breakfast is self-service and eaten around a communal table in the homely dining-room. Bedrooms are simply furnished and full of character, reflecting what a recent visitor confirmed is the main and rare attribute of the place – that of a simple but well-run hotel which gives no hint of being anything other than a cultivated family house. A recent visitor was impressed overall, but had reservations about the home-made food and wine; another commented on the state of the swimming pool.

~

NEARBY Prato; Florence (20 km).
LOCATION in narrow street in Bisenzio river valley, 4 km NE of Prato, (keep parallel with river and train tracks on your left); car parking and grounds
FOOD breakfast
PRICE rooms €€
ROOMS 12 double, one family room; all have bath or shower; central heating; some have phone
FACILITIES dining-room, sitting-room, TV room, gymnasium, terrace, pool
CREDIT CARDS not accepted **CHILDREN** welcome; cots and high chairs by arrangement
DISABLED not suitable **PETS** not usually accepted **CLOSED** never
LANGUAGES English, French **PROPRIETORS** Rucellai Piqué family

SIENA

CASTELLINA IN CHIANTI

BELVEDERE DI SAN LEONINO
～ COUNTRY HOTEL ～

S. Leonino, Castellina in Chianti 53011 Siena
TEL (0577) 740887 **FAX** (0577) 740924

TOURISM HAS BEEN booming in Chianti over the past few years, especially in the commune of Castellina. It is easy to see why: rolling countryside liberally sprinkled with villas, the great art cities within driving distance and a surplus of farmhouses left by people migrating to the cities.

San Leonino is a typical case: a squat, square 15thC house with its barn and stables, built from the light-coloured local stone. The farmyard has been turned into a garden. A tree-shaded terrace has been created at the back, right at the edge of the vineyards, and tucked away out of sight is the swimming-pool. The restoration of the interiors has been meticulously done so that it is difficult to believe that the house is more than five hundred years old.

Sitting areas have been created out of the stables: wide, open rooms spanned by crescent-shaped brick arches. If we have one complaint, it is that the furnishing here would be more suitable for an airport lounge than a Tuscan farmhouse: the long, anonymous modern couches clash badly with the rustic ambience. Bedrooms are of a much higher standard. Prices are good value for this area.

～

NEARBY Siena (15 km); San Gimignano (30 km); Florence (50 km).
LOCATION 15 km N of Siena, in its own grounds; car parking
FOOD breakfast, dinner, lunch on request
PRICE €€
ROOMS 28 double, all with bath or shower, phone
FACILITIES sitting-room, restaurant, bar, terrace, gardens, swimming-pool
CREDIT CARDS AE, EC, MC, V
CHILDREN welcome
DISABLED not suitable
PETS not accepted **CLOSED** mid-Nov to mid-Mar
LANGUAGES English, French, German
PROPRIETOR Marco Orlandi

SIENA

IL COLOMBAIO
∽ COUNTRY HOTEL ∽

Via Chiantigiana 29, Castellina in Chianti 53011 Siena
TEL (0577) 740444 **FAX** (0577) 740444

A NEW ADDITION to the typically Tuscan farmhouse hotels that cluster around Castellina in Chianti, Il Colombaio is a successful example of a proven formula, and at a very reasonable price. As you come from Greve in Chianti on the busy Chiantigiana road (SS 222), you will notice on the right this farmhouse surrounded by lawns, shrubs and trees. Stone-built and capped with the tiled roofs at odd angles to one another so character-istic of Tuscany, the house has a pleasing aspect. It is, however, close to the road.

The restoration has been carried out with attention to detail, using country furniture to complement the rustic style of the building. The sit-ting-room, which used to be the farm kitchen, is spacious and light with beamed ceilings, a traditional open fireplace and, in the corner, the old stone sink now filled with house-plants. Breakfast is served in a small stone-vaulted room on the terrace.

Fifteen of the bedrooms are in the main house (the other six are in an annex across the road) and have been furnished with wrought-iron beds and old-fashioned dressing tables; all have modern bathrooms..

∽

NEARBY Siena (20 km); Florence (40 km); San Gimignano (30 km).
LOCATION just N of Castellina, in own grounds; car parking
PRICE €€
ROOMS 21 double, all with bath or shower
FACILITIES sitting-room, breakfast-room, garden, swimming-pool
CREDIT CARDS AE, DC, EC, MC V
CHILDREN welcome
DISABLED some facilities
PETS please check first **CLOSED** never
LANGUAGES English, French, German
MANAGER Roberta Baldini

SIENA

CASTELLINA IN CHIANTI

PALAZZO SQUARCIALUPI
～ TOWN HOTEL ～

Via Ferruccio, 26 Castellina in Chianti 53011 Siena
TEL (0577) 741186 **FAX** (0577) 740386

PALAZZO SQUARCIALUPI is set right in the heart of the Medieval village of Castellina in Chianti, and when our reporter first visited, she was struck by the friendly, peaceful atmosphere and the lovely rooms.

It is a 14thC stone building with arched doors and windows, which was formerly an imposing farm residence. It has been renovated in a simple, stylish way, while retaining its traditional farm character. There are seventeen large bedrooms and suites with plain white walls, beamed ceilings and dark wooden furniture; downstairs is a rustic sitting-room in muted tones of white, cream and terracotta, and another elegant room with frescoes.

Palazzo Squarcialupi is bound to delight those with an interest in sampling the local wine. Chianti Classico continues to be produced in the Fattoria, and barrels of 'La Castellina', the house wine, line the stone-vaulted cellar. Guests can taste the vintages in the bar or in the wine-tasting room, or on the terrace while admiring magnificent views of the Chianti countryside. New to the guide: reports welcome.

～

NEARBY Siena (18 km); Florence (40 km); San Gimignano (30 km).
LOCATION in town centre, overlooking valley
FOOD buffet breakfast; light meals in the bar
PRICE €€-€€€
ROOMS 9 double; 8 suites; all with bath or shower; all rooms have phone, TV, mini-bar, central heating, air-conditioning
FACILITIES breakfast-room, 2 sitting-rooms, bar, terrace, garden, pool, wine cellar
CREDIT CARDS MC, V
CHILDREN welcome; cradle and cots free
DISABLED 2 suitable rooms
PETS small pets accepted
CLOSED mid-Jan to mid-Mar
LANGUAGES English, French, German, Spanish
PROPRIETORS Targioni family

SIENA

LE PIAZZE
~ CUNTRY HOTEL ~

Le Piazze, Castellina in Chianti, 53011 Siena
TEL (0577) 743190 **FAX** (0577) 743191

A WELCOME ADDITION to the booming hotel scene in the area around Castellina in Chianti which, we feel, has the edge on many of its competitors. Although only 6 km from the bustling town, the hotel is in completely secluded countryside reached by a long unsurfaced road which seems to go on forever the first time around.

The hotel is, needless to say, a converted 17thC farmhouse, but in this case the owners have deployed more imagination and a greater sense of elegance than usual. The buffet breakfast, for instance, is served on tiled sideboards in a room adjacent to the kitchen and separated from it by a glass partition. Or you can remove yourself to any of the numerous terraces that surround the house for uninterrupted views of classical Chianti countryside.

Rustic antiques have, of course, been used in the furnishing with the usual terracotta/exposed beam/white plaster, but with the interesting idea of adding pieces from Indonesia. Bedrooms are individually furnished with lavish use of striped fabrics (avoid those in the roof space – they can become unbearably hot); bathrooms are large, with Jacuzzis or walk-in showers big enough for a party.

~

NEARBY Siena (27 km); Florence (50 km).
LOCATION 6 km W of Castellina in its own grounds; ample car parking
FOOD breakfast
PRICE €€€–€€€€
ROOMS 15 double, all with bath or shower, phone
FACILITIES sitting-room, breakfast-room, bar, terrace, gardens, swimming-pool
CREDIT CARDS AE, DC, EC, MC, V **CHILDREN** over 12s welcome
DISABLED one adapted room
PETS non-barking dogs **CLOSED** never
LANGUAGES English, French, German
PROPRIETOR Maureen Skelly Bonini

SIENA

CASTELLINA IN CHIANTI

SALIVOLPI
~ COUNTRY HOTEL ~

Via Fiorentina, Castellina in Chianti, 53011 Siena
TEL (0577) 740484 **FAX** (0577) 740998

WE REMAIN PLEASANTLY SURPRISED by the excellent value offered by the
Salivolpi in this popular part of Chianti. Prices for a double have not
increased significantly, a sure sign of high advance bookings and a satis-
fied clientèle that returns year after year. Not that this country guest-
house in any way resembles a cheap alternative. Of the many converted
farmhouses in the area, Salivolpi has the edge not just in terms of price
but also because of its pleasant grounds and its swimming-pool.

The buildings consist of the low stone farmhouses typical of Chianti,
surrounded by lawns dotted with flower-beds and terracotta urns. The
thick walls and stone windows are designed to keep out the intense summer sun and an astute use of space and simple, white walls prevents any
sensation of gloominess.

Most of the furniture in the common areas and bedrooms is rustic
antique with a few non-intrusive modern pieces; those in the older building are more characteristic. The whole place is watched over by a professional and attentive staff. Breakfast is the only meal served but there is no
shortage of good restaurants in the vicinity.

~

NEARBY Siena (21 km); San Gimignano (31 km); Florence (45 km).
LOCATION 500m outside town, on road to San Donato in Poggio; own grounds;
ample car parking
FOOD breakfast
PRICE €–€€
ROOMS 19 double, all with bath or shower, phone
FACILITIES sitting-room, breakfast-room, gardens, swimming-pool
CREDIT CARDS MC, V **CHILDREN** welcome
DISABLED one adapted room
PETS not accepted **CLOSED** never
LANGUAGES English, German, French
PROPRIETOR Angela Orlandi

SIENA

TENUTA DI RICAVO
~ COUNTRY HOTEL ~

Loc. Ricavo 4, Castellina in Chianti 53011 Siena
Tel (0577) 740221**Fax** (0577) 741014
E mail ricavo@ricavo.com

LIKE TUSCAN COOKING, the secret of Tenuta di Ricavo's success is easy to describe but difficult to reproduce: simple local ingredients of the highest quality, artfully combined. Here at Ricavo, all the essential elements are present: a hamlet of small stone houses strung out along a hillside, attentive Swiss-Italian owners, and the well-tried formula of a country hotel in the heart of Chianti. The centre of the hamlet is a gravel piazza divided along the diagonal by a row of cypresses. On one side is the main house which now contains the restaurant, sitting-rooms and some of the bedrooms. On the other side of the cypresses are the former farm buildings and peasant dwellings. The hamlet stretches back some distance, so there is no danger of guests crowding in on one another. Furnishing and decoration are of the highest standards. Bedrooms in the main house are more spacious and formal; the others have more individual character, and many have terraces looking on to the wooded valley. The bathrooms have all been recently re-done, and there is a new swimming-pool. One of the finest hotels in the Chianti region – and with a top-class restaurant too.

~

NEARBY Siena (22 km); Florence (45 km).
LOCATION 1 km N of Castellina in Chianti; own car parking
FOOD breakfast, lunch, dinner
PRICE €€€-€€€€
ROOMS 2 single, 13 double, 8 suites all with bath or shower, phone; TV, safe, minibar; 3-day minimum stay in high season
FACILITIES sitting-rooms, bar, restaurant, terrace, 2 swimming-pools, table tennis,
CREDIT CARDS MC, V **CHILDREN** quiet ones
DISABLED no special facilities; some rooms on ground floor
PETS not accepted **CLOSED** Nov to Easter; restaurant only Tue, Wed; Mon-Thu lunch (summer)
LANGUAGES English, French, German **PROPRIETOR** Christina Lobrano-Scotoni

SIENA

CASTELLINA IN CHIANTI

VILLA CASALECCHI
～ COUNTRY VILLA ～

Casalecchi, Castellina in Chianti, 53011 Siena
TEL (0577) 740240 **FAX** (0577) 741111

THIS 18THC VILLA stands on a series of hillside terraces between woods and vineyards, just south of Castellina. The house is no architectural gem, but its secluded position and attractive location compensate for a certain austerity of style in the exteriors. Originally used as a hunting lodge (witness the hallway hung with trophies), the interiors are furnished with heavy, bourgeois antiques which give a hushed character that you might expect visiting the home of an eminent Victorian. The dining-room is frescoed with elegant old light fittings, but a more pleasant place to eat is the terrace with its views of open countryside. Bedrooms are either in the villa (individually furnished), or in the extension, with access to the gardens and pool. Parquet floors and a lighter style of antique makes them more convivial than the public rooms.

The terraces are attractive and well-tended, exploiting their prime location. Some are dotted with flower-filled pots. Down a level is the swimming-pool and below that another terrace, on the edge of the vineyard, where you can lie on a comfortable sun bed. For the energetic, the glories of Chianti are on the doorstep.

～

NEARBY Florence (40 km); Siena (20 km).
LOCATION one km S of Castellina in own grounds; ample car parking
FOOD breakfast, lunch, dinner
PRICE €€€-€€€€
ROOMS 23 double, all with shower or bath, phone, TVr
FACILITIES sitting-rooms, breakfast-room, dining-room, bar, swimming-pool, tennis-court, bowls
CREDIT CARDS AE, DC, EC, MC, V **CHILDREN** welcome
DISABLED no special facilitiesr
PETS accepted but not in public rooms **CLOSED** Oct to Mar
LANGUAGES English, French, German
PROPRIETOR Elvira Lecchini-Giovannoni

SIENA

CASTELNUOVO BERARDENGA

RELAIS BORGO SAN FELICE
~ HILLTOP VILLAGE ~

Loc. Borgo San Felice, Castelnuovo Berardenga 53019 Siena
TEL (0577)359260 **FAX** (0577)359089
E MAIL borgosfelice@

LARGER THAN MOST of the entries in the guide, Borgo San Felice can legitimately be included because this carefully renovated hilltop hamlet is like a collection of charming small hotels. Surrounded by cypresses and the vineyards of the renowned San Felice estate, the tranquil village has the air of being suspended in time. No intrusive neon signs, no lines of cars, just the original Tuscan qualities of perfectly proportioned space setting off simple buildings of brick and stone and topped by a jumble of terracotta roofs. Even the swimming-pool (which can often resemble a gaping, blue gunshot wound) has been discreetly tucked away. Gravel paths, carved well-heads, pergolas, lemon trees in gigantic terracotta pots, a church, a bell-tower and a chapel – one is in the presence of the essence of Tuscany.

All the original features of the various buildings have been retained: vaulted brick ceilings, imposing fireplaces, old tiled floors. The furniture is a stylish mixture of old and modern and the sitting-rooms are full of intimate alcoves. An elegant restaurant completes the picture. Top of the range – and so are the prices.

~

NEARBY Siena (21 km).
LOCATION 21 km NE of Siena in former estate village; ample car parking
FOOD breakfast, lunch
PRICE €€€€
ROOMS 12 suites, 27 double, 6 single; all with bath or shower, phone, TV, minibar
FACILITIES swimming-pool, tennis courts, bowls court, billiards room, conference rooms, sitting-rooms, beauty centre, gym (small)
CREDIT CARDS AE, DC, MC, V **CHILDREN** welcome
DISABLED difficult
PETS no **CLOSED** Nov to March
LANGUAGES English, French, Spanish and German
MANAGER Lorenzo Righi

SIENA

CASTELNUOVO BERARDENGA

PODERE SAN QUIRICO
~ FARM GUEST-HOUSE ~

Via del Paradiso 1 Castelnuovo Berardenga, 53019 Siena
TEL (0577) 355206 **FAX** (0577) 355206

GUESTS RECEIVE a real Neapolitan welcome from Maria Consiglio Picone. The first thing she did when we arrived, on a hot July day, was rush into her kitchen and make us some some freshly squeezed peach juice. From that moment on, she could do no wrong.

The house is a slightly battered relic from the 14thC, built of the local light-coloured stone, with an arched entrance and small, brown-shuttered windows. Terracotta pots filled with flowering plants are dotted about the forecourt where there are also seats to relax in. Perhaps because of Maria's Neapolitan origins and career as a theatre costume designer, the interiors are decorated with more vivacity than is usual in this part of Tuscany: the walls are festooned with plates and paintings, and a lifetime's collection of bric-a-brac cheerfully clutters up the space.

The bedrooms are less festive but enlivened with colourful fabrics and old rugs strewn on the terracotta floors. Bathrooms are up to the mark. Guest can eat in the numerous restaurants or pizzeria nearby or, if they prefer, a separate kitchen and dining-room is at their disposal. And to do? "Here, we sell silence," says Maria. A reader reports missing bedside lamps, no soap and a sense of slipping standards. Reports especially welcome.

~

NEARBY Siena (20 km).
LOCATION 20 km E of Siena, just outside Castelnuovo Berardenga, in own grounds; car parking
FOOD breakfast on request
PRICE €
ROOMS 7 double all with private bathroom; 2 apartments, for 3 or 5 people (L-LLr
FACILITIES breakfast-room, garden with barbecue, kitchen/dining-room
CREDIT CARDS not accepted **CHILDREN** welcome (free for under-fives)
DISABLED not suitable **PETS** not accepted **CLOSED** never
LANGUAGES English
PROPRIETOR Maria Consiglio Picone

SIENA

CASTELNUOVO BERARDENGA

VILLA CURINA
~ COUNTRY VILLA ~

Loc. Curina, Castelnuovo Berardenga, 53019 Siena
TEL (0577) 355586**FAX** (0577) 355412

A VIVACIOUS, convivial atmosphere pervades this hotel-and-apartment complex set in low, rolling countryside north of Siena; when we visited, it was full of activity with people enjoying themselves in the pool, playing tennis or going out for bike rides. In fact, some may find it too energetic for their requirements.

The main villa, surrounded by ornamental gardens and trees, is a large, cream-coloured, 18thC building and contains the bedrooms for guests as well as the principal public rooms. Most of the apartments are in three old stone farmhouses with small, brown-shuttered windows and connected by pathways of Siena brick.

The bedrooms are furnished in a slightly heavier version of the standard rustic manner, but they are all comfortable and well-lit. An attractive restaurant, spanned by strong brick arches, serves fresh produce from the estate along with its own wine and grappa.

Terraced gardens covered with a profusion of flowers and geometric box-hedges lead down from the side of the villa to the swimming-pool and its large, terracotta-paved solarium. A quieter, shadier gravel terrace can be found at the back.

~

NEARBY Castelnuovo Berardenga (6 km); Siena (20 km).
LOCATION 6 km W of Castelnuovo Berardenga in its own grounds; ample car parking
FOOD breakfast, dinner
PRICE €-€€
ROOMS 15 doubles, all with bath or shower, phone, TV; 12 apartments for 2-6 persons
FACILITIES restaurant, terrace, gardens, bikes, swimming-pool, tennis
CREDIT CARDS EC, MC,V **CHILDREN** welcome **DISABLED** no special facilities
PETS not accepted **CLOSED** Nov to Mar/Apr **LANGUAGES** English, German, French
MANAGER Franco Sbardelati

SIENA

CETONA

LA FRATERIA
~ FORMER CONVENT ~

Convento di San Francesco, Cetona, 53040 Siena
TEL (0578) 238015 **FAX** (0578) 239220

ONE OF THE MORE UNUSUAL entries in this guide and not a hotel in the strict sense but a place of hospitality run by a community that has withdrawn from the world. The buildings, grouped around a hillside church founded in 1212 by St. Francis, constructed out of light, golden stone, form a rambling complex. Only seven rooms and suites are available, so, even when it is fully booked, one never has the sensation of being in a busy hotel but a place of retreat. There is no swimming-pool and none of the rooms has a television.

This may sound monastic, but the setting and furnishings are of the same standard as a top-class hotel: antiques, paintings and colourful wooden carvings (generally religious in theme) and spacious rooms with stone and beige stucco walls. The restaurant is unexpectedly sophisticated (and expensive), serving a mixture of refined and hearty food using fresh produce from the gardens.

A stroll around the monastery with its church and chapel, cloisters and courtyards, and hushed, tranquil air will help you realize why the young people of this community want to share their peace.

~

NEARBY Pienza (40 km); Montepulciano (26 km); Montalcino (64 km); Siena (89 km).
LOCATION restored monastery 26 km S of Montepulciano in own grounds; ample car parking
FOOD breakfast, lunch, dinner
PRICE ⓔⓔⓔⓔ
ROOMS 5 double, 2 suites, all with bath or shower, heatingr
FACILITIES sitting-rooms, restaurant, terrace, garden
CREDIT CARDS AE, EC, MC, V **CHILDREN** welcome
DISABLED no special facilities
PETS not accepted **CLOSED** Jan; restaurant only, Tue in winter **LANGUAGES** English
MANAGER Maria Grazia Daolio

SIENA

CHIANCIANO TERME

LA FOCE
~ COUNTRY APARTMENTS ~

Strada della Vittoria 63, 53042 Chianciano Terme (Siena)
TEL AND FAX 0578 69101
E MAIL lafoce@ftbcc.it

ANYONE WHO IS FAMILIAR with the writing of Iris Origo will be particular interested in La Foce, the estate whose history during the Second World War is so vividly described in her book War in the Val d'Orcia. Iris died in 1988, but her family still live on the property in this remote but strangely beautiful corner of Tuscany, and run it as a working farm.

Several of the buildings on the large estate have been converted to into superior self-catering accommodation, ranging from the delightful two-person Bersagliere to the superb and quite grand Montauto which sleeps ten; the latter stands in its own extensive garden with lavender borders and small pool.

Furnishings throughout the comfortable apartments are in sophisticated and tasteful country style, predominantly antique, but with a few well-chosen modern pieces. There is plenty of colour, provided by bright rugs, cushions and cheerful fabrics. Each has its own piece of private garden and the use of a pool. Music lovers will appreciate the excellent chamber music festival which takes place on the estate each July.

~

NEARBY Pienza (20 km); Montepulciano (10 km).
LOCATION 5 km SW of Chianciano Terme. Follow the signs for Monte Amiata and Cassia; own car parking.
FOOD dinner on request
PRICE €€€€€
ROOMS 9 self-catering apartments/houses sleeping 2-10, all with bath and shower, phone, TV on request, central heating r
FACILITIES pools, tennis, playground
CREDIT CARDS not accepted **CHILDREN** welcome
DISABLED 2 adapted rooms
PETS not accepted**CLOSED** never
LANGUAGES English, French, German
PROPRIETORS Benedetta and Donata Origo

SIENA

GAIOLE IN CHIANTI

CASTELLO DI TORNANO
~ COUNTRY APARTMENTS ~

Loc. Lecchi, Gaiole in Chianti, 53013 Siena
TEL (0577) 746067; (055) 6580918 (bookings) **FAX** (0577) 746067; (055) 6580918 (bookings)
E MAIL castellotornano@chiantinet.it **WEB SITE** www.chiantinet.it/castelloditornano

ONE OF THE COUNTLESS defence and watch towers that dot Tuscany, solidly built of grey stone in positions with commandng views of the surrounding countryside, many of them in line of sight with their neighbours. Here, you find yourself in one of the wilder parts of Chianti with views of steep wooded hills, bleak in winter and, even in summer, with an air of inviolable isolation.

Most of the apartments are in a farmhouse adjoining the base of the thousand-year-old tower, and each has a living room with a kitchen area, and one or two bedrooms, furnished in a rustic style, deployed in a relatively simple manner. Some of the apartments are in the tower, and these are decorated with a more studied elegance. Each has its own entrance and a private outdoor area.

The swimming-pool is in a common area and, fittingly for the location, has been fashioned from the remains of the former moat, still spanned by a wooden bridge. Nearby is a small fishing lake and, at the bottom of the hill, a typical Tuscan trattoria. Produce from the estate (wine, oil, vinegar, cheese, eggs and salami) can be bought on the spot.

~

NEARBY Siena (16 km); Florence (50 km).
LOCATION 5 km S of Gaiole;own grounds, ample car parking
FOOD self-catering apartments; family trattoria nearby
PRICE €-€€
ROOMS 9 fully equipped apartments for 2-6 persons
FACILITIES bar, gardens; cleaners on request; swimming-pool, tennis
CREDIT CARDS AE, DC MC, V **CHILDREN** welcome
DISABLED 1 apartment suitable for disabled
PETS small, on request
CLOSED never
LANGUAGES English, French, some German
Manager Barbara Sevolini

SIENA

LECCHI IN CHIANTI

SAN SANO
⮜ COUNTRY VILLAGE HOTEL ⮞

Loc. San Sano, Lecchi in Chianti, 53010 Siena
TEL (0577) 746130 **FAX** (0577) 746156

THE MEDIEVAL HAMLET of San Sano, a clutter of stone houses with uneven terracotta roofs, has at its heart an ancient defence tower, destroyed and rebuilt many times. Now, in its latest incarnation, this imposing structure forms the core of a delightful, family-run hotel in a relatively little visited, authentic part of Chianti.

The various buildings surrounding the tower (which houses some of the bedrooms; others have direct access to the grounds) give the hotel a rambling character, connected by narrow passageways, steep stairways and unexpected courtyards. The restoration has been meticulous and restrained. The decoration is in classic, rustic Tuscan style but with individual touches: carefully chosen antiques, colourful pottery and plenty of flowers. The dining-room, in the former stables, spanned by a massive stone arch and still with the feeding trough, is a cool haven from the summer sun. Each bedroom has its individual character (one with nesting birds in its perforated walls, now glassed off) and gleaming, almost surgical bathrooms. Outside is a stone-paved garden at the foot of the tower and, at a slight remove, a hillside swimming-pool.

NEARBY Radda in Chianti (9 km); Siena (25 km); Florence (60 km).
LOCATION hill-top hamlet in middle of countryside; own car parking
FOOD text breakfast, dinner
PRICE €€€
ROOMS textr 11 doubles, 2 single, all with bath or shower, phone, central heating
FACILITIES sitting-areas, breakfast and dining-room, garden, swimming-pool
CREDIT CARDS AE, DC, EC, MC, V **CHILDREN** welcome
DISABLED one adapted room; ground-floor rooms accessible
PETS please check first **CLOSED** mid-Nov to mid-Mar
LANGUAGES English, German, French, Spanish
PROPRIETORS Giancarlo and Heidi Matarazzo

SIENA

MONTEFOLLONICO

LA CHIUSA
~ COUNTRY GUEST HOUSE ~

Address
TEL 0000 **FAX** 0000
E-MAIL ferme.du.vert@wanadoo.fr **WEBSITE** www.fermeduvert.com

QUITE A FEW of the better small hotels in this guide started off as restaurants and over the years have converted a few rooms for overnight visitors, with such success that they have extended this side of their activities. But in general it is true to say that the restaurant remains the centre of the enterprise. Not that at La Chiusa, a stone farmhouse and frantoio (olive-press), the comfort of guests is secondary. The greatest care and attention has been given to the bedrooms and suites: elegant and spacious, each has been individually furnished with antiques. Colourful rugs cover the old terracotta tiles and modern lamps provide artful lighting. Bathrooms are among the best we have seen, some with hydro-massage and one incorporating old millstones.

Dania Masotti is justifiably proud of her achievements as a cook, and meals in the elegant (and pricey) restaurant are gastronomic experiences that venture beyond the merely regional, despite being based on home ingredients from the farm and vegetable garden. Even the bread served at breakfast is baked on the premises. Extensive gardens, filled with fragrant rosemary and lavender.

~

NEARBY Montepulciano(10 km); Pienza (10 km).
LOCATION 10 km NW of Montepulciano; in own grounds, ample car parking
FOOD breakfast, lunch, dinner
PRICE €€€€-€€€€€
ROOMS 6 double, 5 suites, all with bath, phone, TV, minibar; 3 apartments
FACILITIES sitting-room, restaurant, garden
CREDIT CARDS AE, DC, MC, V **CHILDREN** welcome
DISABLED one adapted room
PETS accepted **CLOSED** Jan to Mar; restaurant only, Jan to Mar, Tue
LANGUAGES English, French, German
PROPRIETORS Dania Masotti and Umberto Lucherini

SIENA

MONTERIGGIONI

MONTERIGGIONI
∼ VILLAGE HOTEL ∼

Via 1 Maggio 4, Monteriggioni, 53035 Siena
TEL (0577) 305009, 305010 FAX (0577) 305011

VISITORS TO TUSCANY have been increasingly keen to drop by well-preserved, medieval Monteriggioni and spend a couple of hours relaxing in the piazza (where a bar serves snacks), browsing the antique shops or sampling the menu of Il Pozzo, one of the finest restaurants in the Siena area. Finally, somebody had the bright idea that a small hotel would not go amiss, especially since the town is peaceful and well placed for exploring the locality.

A couple of old stone houses were knocked together and converted with sure-handed lightness of touch to make this attractive hotel. The former stables now make a large, light and airy public area used as reception, sitting-room and breakfast-room.

At the back, a door leads out to a well-tended garden running down to the town walls and containing what it possibly the smallest swimming-pool in Tuscany. The bedrooms are perfectly acceptable, furnished to a high rustic-antique standard with stylish hyper-modern bathrooms.

∼

NEARBY Siena (10 km); San Gimignano (18 km); Florence (55 km); Volterra (40 km).
LOCATION within the wallsof Monteriggioni, 10 km N of Siena; car parking available outside the walls
FOOD breakfast
PRICE ©©-©©©
ROOMS 2 single, 10 double, all with bath or shower, phone, TV, minibar, air-conditioning
FACILITIES sitting area,breakfast-room, bar, garden,small swimming-pool
CREDIT CARDS AE, DC, EC, MC, V
CHILDREN welcome DISABLED no special facilities
PETS accepted, but check first CLOSED Jan to Feb
LANGUAGES English, French,German
MANAGER Michela Gozzi

SIENA

MONTERIGGIONI

SAN LUIGI
~ COUNTRY HOTEL ~

Loc. Strove, Via della Cerreta 38, Monteriggioni, 53030 Siena
TEL (0577) 301055 **FAX** (0577) 301167

THERE HAS BEEN NO SKIMPING or cutting corners in the conversion of the farm buildings of San Luigi to a country hotel with a difference, which we think will appeal to some readers, especially those travelling with a young family. A long, unpaved drive takes you through acres of grounds to the main building and reception. When we remarked on how green everything was, even in summer, we learned that this was originally an Etruscan settlement and that they always chose areas with supplies of underground water.

Certainly, the present owners of San Luigi have exploited the lush setting. The park is crammed with things to do: swimming, tennis, volleyball, basketball, bowls, even a giant chessboard. If lively group activity is not for you, there are acres of countryside for rambles and secluded corners to retreat to with a book.

It would be unfair to describe San Luigi as a holiday camp, but it would be equally misleading to recommend it to readers in search of a tranquil break. Guests, when we visited, seemed incredibly active – especially the younger ones – and copious buffet meals helped to fuel their energies.

NEARBY Monteriggioni (5 km); Siena (12 km); Florence (50 km).
LOCATION 5 km NW of Monteriggioni in its own spacious park; ample car parking
FOOD breakfast, lunch, dinner
PRICE €€€
ROOMS 2 single, 32 double, 5 apartments for 2-6 people, all with bath or shower
FACILITIES sitting-room, restaurant, bar, gardens, tennis, volley- and basket-ball, 2 swimming-pools, giant chess
CREDIT CARDS AE, DC, EC, MC, V **CHILDREN** welcome
DISABLED 2 rooms specially fitted
PETS small dogs accepted **CLOSED** never
LANGUAGES English, French, German, Spanish
PROPRIETOR Sig. Michelagnoli

Siena

MONTICHIELLO

L'OLMO
~ COUNTRY GUEST HOUSE ~

53020 Montichiello di Pienza, Siena
TEL 0578 755133 **FAX** 0578 755124
WEB SITE www.nautilus-mp.com/olmo

THE INITIAL IMPRESSION given by this solid stone building set on a hillside overlooking the rolling hills of the Val d'Orcia towards Pienza is a little stark. A few trees would soften the lines.Once inside, however, the elegant, comfortable sitting-room, with its Oriental rugs, low beamed ceiling, antiques and glass-topped coffee table laden with books dispel any such feeling. When we visited, there was a fire roaring in the grate and Mozart playing softly in the background.

The spacious bedrooms and suites (two of which have fireplaces) are individually and stylishly decorated in smart country style with floral fabrics, fresh white cotton bedcovers, botanical prints, soft lighting and plenty of plants and dried flowers. One room has the floor-to-ceiling brick-grilled wall (now glassed in) that is so typical of Tuscan barns. The wrought-iron fixtures throughout are by a local craftsman. Two suites have private terraces leading on to the large garden.

The pool has a wonderful view and the arched courtyard makes a pleasant spot for an aperitif.

~

NEARBY Siena (50 km); Pienza (7 km); Montepulciano (12 km).
LOCATION 7 km S of Pienza; follow signs to Montichiello; own car parking
FOOD breakfast, dinner on request
PRICE ⓔⓔⓔ-ⓔⓔⓔⓔ
ROOMS 1 double, 5 suites and 1 self-catering apartment, all with bath and shower, phone, minibar, TV, hairdryer, safe
FACILITIES garden, terraces, pool
CREDIT CARDS AE, EC, MC, V **CHILDREN** welcome
DISABLED one ground floor bedroom
PETS not accepted
CLOSED mid Nov-1 April
LANGUAGES French, English
PROPRIETOR Loredana Lindo

SIENA

PIENZA

IL CHIOSTRO DI PIENZA
∼ FORMER MONASTERY ∼

Corso Rossellino 26, Pienza, 53026 Siena
Tel (0578) 748400 **Fax** (0578) 748440

IN THE MODEST WAY of Renaissance popes, Pius II re-named his home town of Corsignano after himself and made it a model of 15thC urban planning. So it is appropriate that the modern tourist-pilgrim should find lodgings in this stylishly converted monastery. The entrance is located at the back of the austere white cloister that gives the hotel its name and on to which half the rooms look; the other half face away, over the serenely magnificent hills of Val d'Orcia.

Many of the original features of the monks' cells have been retained: frescoed, vaulted ceilings and tiled floors. The furniture, however, breaks with monkish antiquity and concentrates on modern comfort without sinning against the character of the building. Bathrooms, though hardly spacious, are fully equipped.

The sitting-rooms, with their old beamed ceilings, and the restaurant, give on to a delightful terrace garden. There could be no more agreeable place for one's evening aperitivo than its tranquil shade before strolling down Pienza'a elegant Corso to the many restaurants around.
∼

NEARBY Palazzo Piccolomini, the Cathedral; Siena (52 km).
LOCATION centre of town next to Palazzo Piccolomini
FOOD breakfast, lunch, dinner
PRICE €€-€€€€
ROOMS 25 double, 2 single, 2 suites; all with bath; all rooms have phone, TV
FACILITIES sitting-rooms, bar, restaurant, garden
CREDIT CARDS AE, DC, MC, V
CHILDREN welcome
DISABLED access difficult
PETS not accepted
CLOSED Nov to March
LANGUAGES English
MANAGER Michela Boneface

SIENA

PIENZA

LA SARACINA
~ COUNTRY GUEST HOUSE ~

Strada Statale 146, 53026 Pienza, Siena
TEL (0578) 748022 **FAX** (0578) 748018
E MAIL saracina@bccmp.com **WEB SITE** www.emmeti.it

BY THE TIME the McCobbs retired from La Saracina to return to the U.S.A. in 1996, they had created an extremely comfortable guest house. With the attention to detail that seems to be characteristic of foreigners who go into business, they turned an old stone farmhouse and its outbuildings, set in glorious countryside, into something special.

A sense of refinement and good taste pervades: the bedrooms, all with their own entrance from out of doors, are spacious and elegant; suites have sitting areas. Antique furnishings mingle well with bright Ralph Lauren fabrics and there is a distinct leaning towards American country style. The luxurious bathrooms are fitted with marble sinks a nd Jacuzzis - several are enormous. Breakfast is served in the winter garden or in a neat breakfast room. There is an attractive swimming-pool surrounded by smooth lawns.

This is an up-market place and quite a challenge for the new, young owner. We are hoping that her fresh approach and her enthusiasm will win through.

~

NEARBY Pienza (7 km); Montepulciano (6 km).
LOCATION 7 km from Pienza on Montepulciano road; on quiet hillside in own grounds with ample parking
FOOD breakfast
PRICE €€€-€€€€€
ROOMS 2 doubles, 3 suites and 1 apartment (with kitchen), all with bath or shower, phone, TV, minibar
FACILITIES breakfast room, garden, swimming pool
CREDIT CARDS AE, EC, MC, V **CHILDREN** welcomer
DISABLED no special facilities, but all rooms are on ground floor
PETS not accepted **CLOSED** never
LANGUAGES English, French
PROPRIETOR Simonetta Vessichelli

SIENA

PIEVESCOLA DI CASOLE D'ELSA

RELAIS LA SUVERA
~ COUNTRY VILLA ~

Loc. Pievescola di Casole d'Elsa, 53030 Siena
TEL (0577) 960 300/1/2/3 **FAX** (0577) 960 220
E MAIL lasuvera@lasuvera.it **WEB SITE** www.lasuvera.it

IN 1507, when Siena gave the castle of Suvera to Pope Julius II, he added an entire Renaissance villa on the same scale. Later, it changed hands many times (belonging once to the film director, Visconti); now it is one of the most extraordinary hotels in Italy.

Stone-built and three storeys high, in a panoramic position, the uncompromising lines of the fortress wing contrast with the delicate arched loggias, the villa's principal façade. To the side stands a 17thC church, and ornamental gardens carved up by precisely aligned gravel paths.

To do justice to the interiors would require a book in itself. A collector's fantasies come true? A display of aristocratic luxury? Or an essay in kitsch? Each room has a theme (the Pope's Room, the Moor's Room, the Ceramics Room) and each theme has been pursued to its limits. Napoleon's Room is furnished in pure Empire style, hung with heavy drapes and contains a portrait of the brooding megalomaniac himself, surmounted by an Imperial Eagle. Rooms in the converted stables are (relatively) simpler and smaller. An elegant restaurant occupies the former olive-press.

~

NEARBY Siena (28 km); Florence (56 km).
LOCATION 28 km W of Siena, in its own grounds; car parking
FOOD breakfast, lunch, dinner
PRICE €€€€
ROOMS 23 doubles, 12 suites, all with bath or shower, TV, phone, air-conditioning
FACILITIES sitting-rooms, breakfast-room, restaurant, swimming-pool, tennis
CREDIT CARDS AE, DC, EC, MC, V
CHILDREN small children welcome
DISABLED not suitable
PETS on request **CLOSED** Nov to Mar
LANGUAGES English, French, German, Spanish
PROPRIETOR Marchese Ricci

SIENA

POGGIBONSI

VILLA SAN LUCCHESE
~ COUNTRY VILLA ~

Via San Lucchese 5, Poggibonsi, 53036 Siena
TEL (0577) 934231 **FAX** (0577) 934729

DO NOT BE PUT OFF by nearby Poggibonsi, which, most people agree, is one of the ugliest towns in Tuscany. Lying halfway between Florence and Siena, visitors take one look at it from the motorway and speed on, or are forced to skirt it on the way to San Gimignano. However, its ugliness is contained, and once outside its environs, you are back in glorious Tuscan countryside, conscious only of cypresses, olives and vines – which is what you will also see from Villa San Lucchese's hilltop.

The villa is an elegant, 15thC cream-coloured building standing in its own park of sculpted hedges and swirling gravel paths. The interiors have been extensively refurbished to the standards of a four-star hotel, with perhaps more attention paid to modern comforts than to original style. Still, plenty of the character of the old villa remains, whether in the reception area with its heavy-beamed ceilings and low arches or in the dining-room's friezes and sloping roof. More colour would have been welcome in the bedrooms which, with their predominantly white tones, lacked vivacity and personality, even if spacious and comfortable.

~

NEARBY Siena (19 km); Florence (36 km); San Gimignano (13 km).
LOCATION 2 km S of Poggibonsi on hilltop in own grounds; car parking
FOOD breakfast, dinner
PRICE €€-€€€
ROOMS 34 double, 2 suites, all with bath or shower, TV, phone, minibar, air-conditioning
FACILITIES sitting-rooms, restaurant, bar, garden, two swimming-pools, tennis courts, bowls
CREDIT CARDS AE, EC, MC, V
CHILDREN welcome
Disabled no special facilities **PETS** not accepted **CLOSED** Mid jan-mid Feb
LANGUAGES English, French, German
MANAGER Marcantonio Ninci

Siena

Radda in Chianti

RELAIS FATTORIA VIGNALE
~ Country hotel ~

Via Pianigiani 15, Radda in Chianti, 53017 Siena
Tel (0577) 738300 **Fax** (0577) 738592

FATTORIA VIGNALE is not only in the heart of Chianti, it was here that in 1924, Baldassare Pianigiani created the famous black rooster symbol and the Consorzio Vino Chianti Classico, which to this day sets the standards for the production of Italy's most famous wine.

The hotel also sets high standards for itself. Under the management of the quietly efficient Silvia Kummer, you should find no unexpected hitches during your stay here. Decoration and furnishing are tasteful and restrained and blend well with the original character of the manor house. The sitting-rooms are subdued in character, with elegant modern sofas and Persian rugs. One is decorated with frescoed panels depicting rural scenes. The bedrooms, including the ones in the annex across the road, are all well furnished in a superior rustic style.

The building is situated on a slope, and while the front resembles a town house, the back, a couple of levels down, is more like a farmhouse. Here, under a leafy pergola, breakfast is served, and a little further away, with the same dramatic views, is the swimming-pool. Everything we look for in a charming small hotel.

NEARBY Siena (28 km); San Gimignano (40 km); Firenze (45 km).
LOCATION just outside village, 28 km N of Siena; own grounds, ample car parking
FOOD breakfast, snacks
PRICE ⓔⓔⓔ-ⓔⓔⓔⓔ
ROOMS 25 double, 4 single, all with bath or shower, phone, TV, heating. 9 of the rooms are in the annex across the roadr
FACILITIES 3 sitting-rooms, breakfast-room, bar, terrace, garden, swimming-pool
CREDIT CARDS AE, EC, MC, V
CHILDREN welcome but preferably quiet ones
DISABLED lift, but no special facilities **PETS** not accepted
CLOSED 8th-26th Dec; 6th Jan-25th Mar **LANGUAGES** English, German, French
MANAGER Silvia Kummer

SIENA

RADDA IN CHIANTI

PODERE TERRENO
~ COUNTRY GUEST-HOUSEE ~

Via Terreno 21, Volpaia, Radda in Chianti, 53017 Siena
TEL (0577) 738312 **FAX** (0577) 738312

AT PODERE TERRENO you will find everything you might expect from a family guest-house in the heart of Chianti: a four-hundred-year- old farmhouse with views of vines and olive groves; delicious home cooking; and a genuinely friendly welcome.

The dining-room on the upper floor is the centre of the house. As well as eating meals together at the long wooden table, guests can relax in front of the huge, traditional fireplace, its wooden mantle hung with cheerful ceramics and mounted antlers. The room is packed full of rural artifacts: burnished copper vessels hang from the wooden beams, a cupboard hollowed out of a tree trunk, shelves stacked with bottles of wine. Downstairs there is another sitting-room. The bedrooms, all off a long corridor, are simply but well furnished, each named after a type of vine, their white plaster walls enlivened with coloured stencils of flowers and plants. Bathrooms are smallish, with slightly garish green tiling.

Come evening, you can take your glass of red to the covered sitting area in the garden and watch the swallows swirling around the terracotta roofs.
~

NEARBY Siena (35 km); Florence (43 km).
LOCATION 5 km N of Radda in Chianti; car parking
FOOD breakfast, dinner
PRICE €€
ROOMS 7 double, 6 with shower, 1 with bath
FACILITIES sitting-room, dining-room, terrace, table-tennis; lake nearby
CREDIT CARDS AE, EC, MC, V
CHILDREN welcome
DISABLED not suitable
PETS accepted
CLOSED never
LANGUAGES English, French, German
PROPRIETORS Marie-Sylvie Haniez and Roberto Melosi

SIENA

RADDA IN CHIANTI

VESCINE - IL RELAIS DEL CHIANTI
∼ HILLTOP HOTEL ∼

Loc. Vescine, Radda in Chianti, 53017 Siena
TEL (0577) 741144 **FAX** (0577) 740263

THERE IS AN ALMOST manicured air to the buildings and gardens of Vescine, a group of perfectly-restored farmhouses strung out along a hillside between Castellina and Radda. Perhaps it is because of the comparatively recent restructuring in 1990 that these medieval buildings look as if they might be a film set. Everything is in perfect order: not a tile out of place, not a weed in the garden. The sitting-rooms are on two levels of an upper floor connected by a stone stairway. The lower one is spacious, with exposed beam ceilings supported by a large white column that divides the room up into various areas including a bar; the upper one is smaller and rather pretentiously called a library on the strength of a few books.

The bedrooms are spread around the various houses (which are connected by brick paths, criss-crossing the terraced gardens) and are in the same pristine style. A little more imagination and fewer hackneyed pictures would have given them more character.

The location of the hotel provides it with panoramic views, especially from the swimming-pool. The restaurant is some distance away and there are plenty of others in the area.

∼

NEARBY Siena (28 km); Florence (42 km).
LOCATION 5 km E of Castellina, just off road to Radda; own grounds, ample car parking
FOOD breakfast; associated restaurant 700m away
PRICE €€€€-€€€€€
ROOMS 16 double, 7 suites, all with bath or shower, phone, TV, minibar
FACILITIES sitting-room, bar, breakfast-room, garden, tennis, swimming-pool
CREDIT CARDS AE, EC, MC, V
CHILDREN welcome
DISABLED no special facilities
PETS dogs accepted**CLOSED** Nov to Mar
LANGUAGES English, French, German
MANAGER Birgit Fleig

SIENA

LA PALAZZINA
~ COUNTRY GUEST-HOUSE ~

Loc. Le Vigne, Celle sul Rigo, Radicofani, 53040 Siena
TEL (0578) 55771 **FAX** (0578) 53553
E MAIL collection@veridea.no

L A PALAZZINA WAS ONCE a restaurant with a few rooms, but it is now a
guest-house with the bonus of excellent in-house dining. Certainly, the
setting is too attractive only to use for a few hours in the evening : a 17thC
hilltop hunting lodge approached by an alley of cypresses in rolling countryside, with manicured gardens and a pristine swimming-pool.

The interiors are more modern than the house's 17thC origins would
lead you to expect, and are due to an unfortunate restructuring by a previous owner. But not all character has been lost and much has been added,
through the judicious use of 19thC antiques and stylishly chosen fabrics.
Black-and-white tiling on the floors makes a welcome change from terracotta and gives a clean, cool look to the rooms. The bedrooms are in a similar style with beamed ceilings and wrought-iron beds; a few have their
own terraces.

The restaurant is still an important part of life at La Palazzina, using
fresh produce from the farm. The cuisine rises above the level of 'local
specialities', and is served to softly playing baroque music in the elegant
restaurant.

~

NEARBY Pienza; Montepulciano (30 km); Montalcino (35 km).
LOCATION 5 km E of Radicofani in its own grounds; ample car parking
FOOD breakfast, dinner
PRICE € room and breakfast; €€ (DB&B per person)
ROOMS 10 double, all with bath or shower; 2 apartments
FACILITIES sitting-room, bar, restaurant, garden, swimming-pool; riding nearby
CREDIT CARDS EC, MC, V
CHILDREN welcome
DISABLED one adapted room
PETS upon request
CLOSED Nov to Mar
LANGUAGES English, French
PROPRIETOR Nicoletta Innocenti

SIENA

SAN CASCIANO DEI BAGNI

SETTE QUERCE
~ VILLAGE GUEST-HOUSE ~

53040 San Casciano dei Bagni, Siena
TEL 0578 58174 **FAX** 0578 58172
E MAIL settequerce@krenet.it **WEB SITE** www.evols.it/settequerce

SEVERAL GENERATIONS of Daniela Boni's family have run the local bar in this tiny spa town, located high in the hills in a remote corner of southern Tuscany. The family business expanded in 1997 to include a delightful and original hotel, and most recently, the bar has extended into an excellent restaurant.

The name derives from the fact that the rambling town house backs on to an oak wood. The contemporary interior design is a refreshing change from the Tuscan norm. At ground level, earth tones, vivid reds and pinks prevail. Bedrooms on the second floor are in sunny yellows and greens, and at the top, shades of blue predominate. The cheerful fabrics on chairs, curtains, cushions and duvets are by Designers Guild. The rooms are all dotted with ornaments (old irons, rustic ceramics, basket ware), while framed black-and-white photos depicting the history of the village decorate the walls. Each bedroom has a comfortable sitting area (compensating for the lack of public sitting room) and a cleverly-designed kitchenette. Bathrooms are immaculate and several have Jacuzzis.

NEARBY thermal baths; Pienza (40km); Orvieto (40 km); Montepulciano (40 km).
LOCATION on street just outside town with ample public car parking close by
FOOD breakfast
PRICE €€€-€€€€€
ROOMS 9 suites, all with bath and shower, phone, TV, air conditioning, minibar
FACILITIES bar, terraces, restaurant (same management, nearby)
CREDIT CARDS AE, EC, MC, V
CHILDREN welcome
DISABLED Two adapted ground-floor suites
PETS accepted if small
CLOSED 2 weeks in Jan
LANGUAGES English, French
PROPRIETORS Daniela, Maurizio and Silvestro Boni

SIENA

SAN GIMIGNANO

L'ANTICO POZZO
~ TOWN GUEST-HOUSE ~

Via San Matteo 87, 53037 San Gimignano, Siena
TEL (0577) 942014 **FAX** (0577) 942117
E MAIL info@anticopozzo.co **WEB SITE** www.anticopozzo.com

THE ANCIENT BRICK WELL in question (pozzo means well) is in the entrance
hall of this fine, 15thC town house situated on one of the pedestrian
streets leading up to San Gimignano's central Piazza del Duomo. The
building was beautifully restored in 1990, and is now, in our view, possibly
the best hotel in town.

A stone staircase leads up to the large first-floor bedrooms and the
breakfast room, the latter known as the sala rosa thanks to its deep pink
walls. The waxed and worn terracotta tiles on this floor are original, as are
the high, beamed ceilings. Several rooms have delicate frescoes; in one,
the walls and ceiling are entirely painted with garlands of flowers and elegant, dancing figures.

Rooms on the upper floors are smaller, but still most attractive. Those
at the top have attic ceilings and views of the famous towers or countryside to compensate for their small size.

Furnishings throughout are in simple good taste; carefully-chosen
antiques mix well with the wrought-iron beds; colours are muted.
Bathrooms are all due to be smartened up this winter. A pretty, walled terrace is an added bonus.

~

NEARBY Cathedral; Museo Civico; Torre Grossa.
LOCATION on pedestrian street in centre of town with public parking (300 m)
FOOD breakfast
PRICE €€€-€€€€
ROOMS 1 single and 17 doubles, all with bath or shower, phone, TV, radio, air
conditioning, minibar
FACILITIES bar, terrace, breakfast room **SMOKING** not permitted in public rooms
CREDIT CARDS AE, DC, EC, MC, V **CHILDREN** welcome
DISABLED 2 adapted rooms and lift **PETS** not accepted
CLOSED 6 weeks in winter **LANGUAGES** English, German, Spanish
PROPRIETOR Emanuele Marro L'Olmo

SIENA

SAN GIMIGNANO

CASALE DEL COTONE
~ COUNTRY GUEST-HOUSE ~

Loc. Cellole 59, San Gimignano, 53037 Siena
TEL (0577) 943236, 941395

AN IMPRESSIVELY RESTORED farmhouse that has been decorated with taste to make it one of the finer bed-and-breakfasts in the San Gimignano area. The house, a long, low building with small brown-shuttered windows and the occasional external stairway, was once used as a hunting lodge and in the breakfast-room are the remains of a fresco depicting a deer in flight and a pheasant.

Great care has been taken with both the interiors and exteriors. Outside are well-tended gardens with gravel paths and neatly kept, colourful flowerbeds, and the house is so positioned that even on a torrid August evening you will catch a cool breeze sitting there. Plans are also afoot to construct a swimming-pool.

On the ground floor is the sitting-room and breakfast area; in fine weather, breakfast is served in the garden. We were impressed with the furniture and decoration, using a few well-chosen antiques to set off the fine proportions of the rooms. The bedrooms have a similar, uncluttered, tasteful ambience, conducive to the peaceful, almost hushed atmosphere. The Casale opened relatively recently, so we would welcome reports.

~

NEARBY Siena (35 km); Florence (50 km); Volterra (28 km).
LOCATION 2 km N of SanGimignano on the road to Certaldo; own grounds, ample car parking
FOOD breakfast, snacks
PRICE €-€€
ROOMS 6 double, 2 apartments, all with bath and shower Facilities sitting-room, bar, garden
CREDIT CARDS not accepted
CHILDREN very young only DISABLED one suitable room
PETS not accepted
CLOSED Nov to Jan
LANGUAGES English, French
PROPRIETOR Alessandro Martelli

SIENA

SAN GIMIGNANO

LE RENAIE
~ COUNTRY HOTEL ~

Loc. Pancole, San Gimignano, 53037 Siena
TEL (0577) 955044 **FAX** (0577) 955126

L E RENAIE IS THE SISTER HOTEL of the nearby Villa San Paolo (page 000) and in some ways might be considered the poor relation, with a more modest approach to furnishing and decoration, but with the advantage of lower prices. The building is no architectural masterpiece, but a typical example of a modern rustic construction: a covered terrace framed by brick arches where, in fine weather, breakfast and dinner are served; French windows that open directly on to the private balconies belonging to some of the bedrooms.

Inside, modern terracotta flooring and cane furniture make for a light, fresh atmosphere. The restaurant, Da Leonetto, is popular with locals (especially for large functions) but gets mixed notices from reporters. Upstairs are the bedrooms which have a mixture of modern, built-in furniture and reproduction rustic.

Guests seem to appreciate the peaceful location, the full range of hotel services (including a swimming-pool and access to the tennis court of Villa San Paolo) and the very reasonable prices. A useful place to base yourself for a few days if you are thinking of combining city touring with days by the swimming-pool.

~

NEARBY San Gimignano (5 km); Siena (38 km); Volterra
LOCATION 6 km N of San Gimignano, off road to Certaldo; private car parking
FOOD breakfast, lunch, dinner
PRICE €-€€
ROOMS 24 double, 1 single, all with bath or shower, phone, TV, air-conditioning, safe, minibar
FACILITIES sitting-area, restaurant, garden, swimming-pool
Credit cards AE, DC, EC, MC, V Children welcome; must be accompanied at swimming-pool **DISABLED** no special facilities **PETS** not in public areas
CLOSED Nov **LANGUAGES** English, German, French
PROPRIETOR Leonetto Sabatini

SIENA

SAN GIMIGNANO

VILLA SAN PAOLO
~ COUNTRY VILLA ~

Strada per Certaldo, SanGimignano, 53037 Siena
TEL (0577) 955100 **FAX** (0577) 955113
WEBSITE http://www.tin.it/san_gimignano

THERE IS AN ALMOST un-Tuscan feel to Villa San Paolo. Not, of course, from the surroundings of cypresses and olives, and with a view of San Gimignano from the swimming-pool: you are in no doubt about where you are. But the villa is not particularly Tuscan in style, and inside, a lightness of touch in the choice of colours and furnishings gives it a welcome individuality and freshness.

On the ground floor are the foyer and public rooms in a pleasant mixture of grey, green and white; modern cane furniture is mixed with antiques. Bedrooms are on the two floors above, and those just below the roof have smallish windows. A common style has been followed with colour co-ordination of carpets, furniture and fabrics. One criticism: in one or two of the bedrooms it may be time to change the carpets. Bathrooms are spanking new with attractive check tiling.

Outside are the well-tended gardens, with gravel paths skirted by curling box-hedges under tall umbrella pines. A small ornamental fountain gurgles soothingly. The swimming-pool has its own bar and a covered terrace where breakfast is served in fine weather.

~

NEARBY San Gimignano (5 km); Siena (38 km).
LOCATION 5 km N of SanGimignano on the road to Certaldo; private car parking
FOOD breakfast, snacks
PRICE €€€-€€€€
ROOMS 18 double all with bath or shower, phone, TV, minibar, safe, air-conditioning
FACILITIES sitting-room breakfast-room, bar, garden,swimming-pool, tennis
CREDIT CARDS AE, DC, EC, MC, V **CHILDREN** welcome
DISABLED adapted rooms available
PETS not accepted
CLOSED 8 Jan to Feb/Mar
LANGUAGES English, French,German
MANAGER Remo Squarcia

SIENA

SAN GUSME

VILLA ARCENO
~ COUNTRY VILLA ~

Loc. Arceno,San Gusme, Castelnuovo Berardenga, 53010 Siena
TEL (0577) 359292 **FAX** (0577) 359276

VILLA ARCENO ORIGINALLY served as a hunting lodge for a Tuscan noble family, but 'lodge' is too humble a word to describe this aristocratic building. A long private road winds through the thousand-hectare estate (which has many farmhouses converted into apartments) to the square, rigidly symmetrical villa with its overhanging eaves, surrounded by lawns, gravel paths and flower-filled terracotta urns. In front of the villa is a separate, walled park in the Romantic style, with shady paths leading down to a small lake.

Inside, a cool, elegant style prevails: off-white walls and vaulted ceilings contrast with the warmth of terracotta floors (strewn with Persian carpets), reproduction antique furniture and light yellow drapes. The atmosphere is formal, but not stiffly so: the highly professional staff make guests feel more than welcome.

Upstairs, the guest-rooms which are all light and spacious, have been individually decorated. Particularly attractive is the suite, which has a bay of three arched windows. Some rooms have their own terraces. You should also ask to see the spiral stairway of the central tower that finishes in a roof-top gazebo.

~

NEARBY Siena (30 km); Florence (90 km).
LOCATION 30 km NE of Siena in its own estate; ample car parking
FOOD breakfast, lunch, dinner
PRICE €€€€-€€€€€
ROOMS 16 double, all with bath, phone, TV, mini-bar, air-conditioning
FACILITIES sitting-rooms, restaurant, gardens, tennis, swimming-pool, bikes
CREDIT CARDS AE, DC, EC, MC, V **CHILDREN** not accepted
DISABLED not suitable **PETS** small dogs, but check first
CLOSED mid-Nov to mid-Mar
LANGUAGES English, French, German
PROPRIETOR Gualtiero Mancini

Siena

Sarteano

Le Anfore
~ Country guest-house ~

Via di Chiusi 30, 53047 Sarteano, Siena.
Tel (0578) 265969 **Fax** (0578) 265521
Web site www.balzarini.it

THE CORNER OF TUSCANY surrounding Sarteano and Cetona is still relatively little visited despite the unspoilt countryside and the increasing number of good places in which to stay and eat. The Pienza/Montepulciano area (still quite close) is much more popular. However, Le Anfore is a useful base for exploring the Val d'Orcia, and prices are reasonable.

It's an old farmhouse, restored without particular flair or style, and, it must be said, the odd lapse of taste: there is a gnome near the front door, and hideous lighting in the downstairs public rooms. However, the atmosphere is pleasantly rustic and relaxed with a huge fireplace in the brick-arched living room.

Bedrooms, named after winning thoroughbreds in the owners' stables, are mostly spacious and a little more stylish than the public rooms, with dark, polished parquet floors and oriental rugs; several have sitting areas. Bathrooms are smartly tiled and well lit.

Outdoors, there is plenty to do, with a big pool in the garden and tennis and riding (of all standards) nearby.

~

Nearby Chianciano terme (14 km); Montepulciano (22 km).
Location 2 km NE of Sarteano on Chiusi road in own grounds with ample parking
Food breakfast, dinner
Price €-€€
Rooms 7 doubles, 3 suites, all with bath or shower, phone, TV, minibar
Facilities sitting room, bar, restaurant, garden, pool; tennis and riding nearby
Credit cards AE, EC, MC, V
Children welcome
Disabled no special facilities
Pets small dogs
Closed 7-30 Nov
Languages German, English
Manager Maurizio Pozielli

SIENA

SIENA

CERTOSA DI MAGGIANO
~ CONVERTED MONASTERY ~

Via Certosa 82, Siena 53100.
TEL (0577) 288180 **FAX** (0577) 288189
E MAIL certosa@relaischateaux.fr

THOUGH IT LIES in the suburbs of Siena, this former Carthusian monastery – the oldest in Tuscany – has the benefit of its own large park and a luxuriously peaceful atmosphere. Although it is expensive, it is not swanky. The emphasis is on calm elegance and discreet service. A star of our all-Italy guide, we feel we can hardly ignore it here.

If the decoration of the bedrooms is disappointing, it is only because they do not live up to the ravishing public rooms. Guests can help themselves to drinks in the book-lined library, play backgammon or chess in a little ante-room or relax in the lovely sitting-room. The fact that this was formerly the family home of the hotel's cultured owners is reflected in the country house atmosphere, with fresh flower arrangements just about everywhere. Excellent modern haute cuisine dishes are served with some ceremony in the pretty dining-room, in the tranquil 14thC cloisters or under the arcades by the swimming-pool.

Bear in mind that you will have to explore Siena by bus – it's too far to walk, and parking is almost impossible in the centre.

~

NEARBY Siena sights; San Gimignano (40 km); Florence (58 km).
LOCATION 1 km SE of city centre and Porta Romana; in gardens, with car parking opposite entrance and garage available
FOOD breakfast, lunch, dinner
PRICE €€€€€
ROOMS 5 double, 12 suites; all with bath; all have central heating, TV, phone, radio
FACILITIES dining-room, bar, library, sitting-room; tennis, heated outdoor swimming-pool, heliport
CREDIT CARDS AE, DC, MC, V
CHILDREN accepted
DISABLED access possible – 3 rooms on ground floor **PETS** not accepted
CLOSED never
MANAGER Margherita Grossi

Siena

SIENA

PALAZZO RAVIZZA
~ TOWN HOTEL ~

Pian dei Mantellini 34, 53100 Siena
TEL (0577) 280462 **FAX** (0577) 221597
E MAIL bureau@palazzoravizza.it

SIENA IS NOTORIOUS for its dearth of decent hotels in the centre of town, so we were delighted to see that Palazzo Ravizza (which has featured in our all-Italy guide for some years) has undergone a facelift and is now a very pleasant place in which to stay. Fortunately, the old fashioned, slightly faded charm has not been sacrificed to modernisation. The bedrooms still have their heavy-at-times quirky period furniture and polished parquet or terracotta floors, but the fabrics have been smartened up and bathrooms are all shining new with heated towel rails. Some even have double Jacuzzis.

Downstairs, the public rooms (in part with smart black-and-white floor tiles) have pretty painted ceilings and comfortable arm chairs and sofas. There is a cosy library, a smart new bar and an elegantly-appointed dining room. The slightly overgrown garden at the back is a great asset providing a cool and shady respite from the city heat, and tables are invitingly laid outside for breakfast and dinner in the summer.

~

NEARBY The Cathedral, Ospedale Santa Maria della Scala.
LOCATION SW of the town centre in residential street with own car parking
FOOD breakfast, dinner
PRICE rooms (€)-(€)(€). Half board, compulsory in high season, add (€)
ROOMS 35 doubles and twins; 5 suites; all with bath or shower, phone, TV, minibar
FACILITIES sitting rooms, bar, restaurant, garden
CREDIT CARDS AE, DC, MC, V
CHILDREN welcome
DISABLED Lift Pets accepted
CLOSED never
LANGUAGES English, French, German
PROPRIETOR Francesco Grotanelli de Santi

SIENA

LOCANDA DELL'AMOROSA
~ COUNTRY INN ~

Sinalunga, 53048 Siena
TEL (0577) 677211**FAX** (0577) 63200
E MAIL mailbox@abitarelastoria.it **WEB SITE** www.abitarelastoria.it

IN A CORNER of the Siena province, which is not overburdened with quality hotels, the Locanda dell'Amorosa shines out. It is as romantic as it sounds: an elegant Renaissance villa-cum-village, within the remains of the 14thC walls.

The accommodation consists of apartments in the houses where peasants and farm-workers once lived, or in the bedrooms in the old family residence. They are cool, airy and pretty, with whitewashed walls, terracotta floors, antique furniture and Florentine curtains and bedspreads – as well as immaculate modern bathrooms.

The old stables, beamed and brick-walled, have been transformed into a delightful rustic (but pricey) restaurant serving modern interpretations of traditional Tuscan recipes, using ingredients from the estate, which also produces wine.

To complete the village, there is a little parish church with a lovely 15thC fresco of the Sienese school. With discreet, attentive service, the Locanda dell'Amorosa remains, in our view, a Mecca for romantics.

~

NEARBY Siena (45 km); Arezzo (45 km); Chianti.
LOCATION 2 km S of Sinalunga, ample car parking
Meals breakfast, lunch, dinne
FOOD breakfast, lunch, dinner
PRICE ©©©©
ROOMS 12 double, 4 suites, all with bathroom; all rooms have central heating, phone, colour TV, minibar, air-conditioning
FACILITIES dining-room, sitting-room, bar
CREDIT CARDS AE, DC, MC, V
CHILDREN accepted
DISABLED access difficult **PETS** not accepted
CLOSED mid-Jan to end Feb; restaurant only, Mon, Tue
MANAGER Carlo Citterio

SIENA

SOVICILLE

BORGO PRETALE
~ HILLSIDE HAMLET ~

Loc. Pretale, Rosia Sovicille, 53018 Siena
Tel (0577) 345401 **Fax** (0577) 345625
E mail borgopret@ftbcc.it

A LONG, WINDING, unsurfaced road through wooded hills brings you to this group of grey stone houses clustered around a massive 12thC watchtower. Local historians claim that it was part of a system of such towers, spread across the Sienese hills, all within line of sight, to communicate quickly any news of approaching invaders and to provide protection against their rampages. Nowadays, this civilized retreat offers a haven from the rampages of modern life.

Every detail has been considered in the restoration and decoration. The harshness of the medieval structure has been lessened by the use of well-chosen antiques, mellow lighting and rich, striped fabrics. A serenely beautiful 15thC carved wooden Madonna, bearing the Infant Christ, stands in a brick-framed niche.

Every bedroom contains a different blend of the same artful ingredients, each splendid in its own individual way, though we particularly liked those in the tower. The stylish restaurant serves a limited choice of dishes (but all well-prepared) and has an extensive wine list on which a sommelier can offer advice. And tucked away, close to the edge of the woods, is an inviting pool.

~

Nearby Siena (20 km); San Gimignano (28 km).
Location 20 km SE of Siena on quiet hillside; own car parking
Food breakfast,, lunch
Price €€€€
Rooms 32 double, 3 suites, all with bath or shower, phone, TV, minibar, air-conditioning
Facilities sitting-room, restaurant, bar, garden, swimming-pool, tennis, sauna, archery
Credit cards all
Children welcome **Disabled** not suitable **Pets** not accepted
Closed 1st Nov to 5th Apr **Languages** English, French German
Director Daniele Rizzardini

SIENA

SOVICILLE

BORGO DI TOIANO
COUNTRY HOTEL

Loc. Toiano, Sovicille, 53018 Siena
TEL (0577) 314639 **FAX** (0577) 314641

MOST OF THE ABANDONED rural hamlets (borgo) that once housed small farming communities and have since been converted into distinctive hotels were, for protection's sake, located on steep hills or jumbled together behind secure walls. Borgo di Toiano, by contrast, has a pleasant open aspect: a few old stone houses, superbly restored, spread out across acres of stone and terracotta terraces, with views over the flat, cultivated valley to low hills on the horizon.

The terraces, to which many of the bedrooms have direct access, are dotted with rosebeds, flower pots and wrought-iron garden furniture, so that breakfast can be enjoyed in the early morning sun. The main public rooms also maintain a spacious, uncluttered feel, with fine antiques and old rugs contrasting with the pristine restoration. Tapestries and modern paintings are set off nicely by the white walls and subtle lighting. The bedrooms maintain the same mixture of rustic and modern with the emphasis on simplicity and comfort, and we particularly recommend those with views.

Below the main group of houses, on the last terrace of this shallow-sloping location, is the swimming-pool.

NEARBY Siena (12 km); San Gimignano (50 km.
LOCATION 12 km SW of Siena in its own grounds; car parking
FOOD breakfast
PRICE €€€-€€€€
ROOMS 7 double, 3 suites, all with shower or bath, phone, TV, minibar, air-conditioning
FACILITIES sitting-room, bar, terraces, garden, swimming-pool
CREDIT CARDS AE, DC, EC, MC, V **CHILDREN** welcome; extra bed in room free
DISABLED some adapted rooms with bathrooms **PETS** accepted **CLOSED** Nov to Mar
LANGUAGES English, French, German
MANAGER Pierluigi Pagni

SIENA

VOLPAIA

LA LOCANDA
~ COUNTRY GUEST-HOUSE ~

Loc. Montanino, 53017 Radda in Chianti, Siena.
TEL AND FAX (0577) 738833
E MAIL info@locanda.com Web site www.lalocanda.it

THE BEVILAQUAS (he, Neapolitan, she Milanese) began their search for the ideal spot in which to set up their guest house four years ago. In April 1999, what was once a collection of ruined farm buildings high up in the Chianti hills finally opened for business, and you would be hard pressed to find a more beautiful setting. At 600 metres above sea level, views from the terraces, garden, pool and some of the rooms are of layers of hills, striped with vines and shaded with woods; in the foreground is the ancient, mellow fortified hamlet of Volpaia.

The restoration of the pale stone buildings has been done with unerring good taste. Interiors, while maintaining many of the rustic features, have a refreshingly contemporary look, with an imaginative use of colour throughout to offset plenty of terracotta and wood. The comfortable bedrooms have an uncluttered feel, and the bathrooms are spacious and gleaming. One end of the long, sunny living room is dominated by a massive stone fireplace, and filled with colourfully-upholstered sofas and arm chairs.

~

NEARBY Florence (48km); Siena (38 km).
LOCATION 4 km west of Volpaia. From piazza in village, follow signs to hotel
FOOD breakfast, dinner on request
PRICE €€€-€€€€
ROOMS 6 doubles and 1 suite, all with bath and shower, phone, TV, and safe.
FACILITIES terraces, garden, swimming- pool
CREDIT CARDS AE, DC, EC, MC, V **CHILDREN** welcome
DISABLED some ground floor bedrooms, but no special facilities
PETS not accepted
CLOSED mid-Jan to mid-March
LANGUAGES English, French
PROPRIETORS Guido and Martina Bevilaqua

PERUGIA

ASPROLI

LA PALAZZETTA
~ COUNTRY GUEST-HOUSE ~

Loc. Asproli, Todi 06050 Perugia
TEL (075) 8853219 **FAX** (075) 8853358 **E-MAIL** 0758853360@iol.it
WEBSITE www.members.it.tripod.de \Marcias\index.html

AT SOME POINT in the 1920s, La Palazzetta must have been an artistic colony, for in many parts of this complex, formed of a villa and its surrounding farmhouses, one comes across remnants of creative activity – especially in the main building, where people often ask to see the frescoes by Dottori & Balla. It is easy to understand what attracted artists to this place: the wonderful Umbrian light which La Palazzetta, with its vistas of rolling green hills, enjoys to the maximum and the sense of community one feels in this compact group of houses, almost a small village. Aids to hedonism include a fine swimming-pool and a restaurant, while for the energetic there are country walks. (In the restaurant, incidentally, one can see evidence of La Palazzetta's artistic tradition in the trompe-l'oeil fresco that covers an entire wall.

Furnishing and decor are of a good standard, although we did not get the opportunity to see the bedrooms in the main villa, said to be a cut above the others, some of which are a bit on the small side. Care has been taken in restoration not to disturb the native character of the original 17thC buildings.

~

NEARBY Todi (8 km); Orvieto (30 km).
LOCATION 8 km SW of Todi, following signs on SS 448,in its own grounds; car parking
FOOD breakfast, lunch, dinner
PRICE €
ROOMS 19 double, all with bath or shower, phone, TV
FACILITIES sitting-room, bar,restaurant, garden, bowls, swimming-pool, archery, mountain bikes Smoking permitted Credit cards EC, MC, V Children welcome
DISABLED no special facilities
PETS please check first
CLOSED Nov to mid-Feb (except Christmas)
LANGUAGES English, French
Proprietor Ensoli Caracciolo Del Leone

PERUGIA

ASPROLI

POGGIO D'ASPROLI
~ COUNTRY GUEST-HOUSE ~

Loc. Asproli 7, 06059 Todi, Perugia
TEL & FAX(075) 8853385

IF YOU ARE TIRED of Naples, you may not be tired of life – just in need of peace and quiet. Such was the case with Bruno Pagliari, so he sold his large southern hotel to continue his career as an artist in the tranquillity of Umbria's leafy valleys. But the tradition of hospitality remained, and he has opened up his hillside farmhouse so that his guests can also enjoy this oasis.

The rambling building of local stone is packed full of an arresting mixture of antiques and Bruno's own modern art. The main sitting-room, with its great fireplace and white couches, is flanked by a long terrace where one can eat or just relax, listening to the birdsong of the wooded hills.

In the rest of the house, stone and brick arches frame decoratively painted doors and parchment-shaded lights illuminate old coloured wooden carvings. The bedrooms will inspire many a pleasant dream.

The atmosphere is hushed, but in a relaxed rather than reverent manner and, birdsong aside, the only sound is of operatic arias gently playing in the background.

~

NEARBY Todi (7 km); Orvieto (29 km).
LOCATION country house in its own grounds
FOOD breakfast; dinner on request
PRICE €€
ROOMS 7 double, 2 suite all with shower or bath, phone, heating
FACILITIES pool, garden, terrace, sitting-room
CREDIT AE, MC, V
CHILDREN not suitable
DISABLED difficult
PETS not accepted
CLOSED Jan to Feb
LANGUAGES English, French, German
PROPRIETOR Bruno Pagliari

PERUGIA

ASSISI

IL MORINO
~ COUNTRY RESTAURANT AND GUEST-HOUSE ~

Via Spoleto 8, Bastia Umbra, 86083 Perugia
TEL & FAX (075) 8010839

STAYING WITHIN THE WALLS of Assisi has become an increasingly unrewarding experience. Parking is almost always difficult, most hotel rooms are costly, and late-night noise has irritated more than a few of our reporters. This attractive restaurant and guest-house stands just outside Assisi, at Bastia Umbra in a patch of green countryside between the city walls and the towns of the Chiascio plain. The Battistelli family's farm has been protected from encroachments of city development by the local green belt policy. Within their oasis, they have tastefully converted their traditional, stone-built farmhouse into a restaurant and guest-house which provide excellent value for travellers on a low budget.

The moderate-sized bedrooms are pleasantly furnished with reproductions of what Signora Battistelli describes as "the style of our grandparents' day". Two rooms have balcony views up to Assisi.

The restaurant is run by an extremely competent chef whose menu, though Umbrian-based, often runs further afield. Many of the ingredients – including poultry, vegetables, fruit and wine – are produced by the family azienda.

~

NEARBY Assisi (2 km); Santa Maria degli Angeli (1 km).
LOCATION 2 km W of Assisi, off SS147; ample parking
FOOD breakfast, lunch, dinner
PRICE rooms €; DB&B €
ROOMS 10 double, with shower and central heating
FACILITIES sitting-room, restaurant, bar; garden, minigolf, bicycles
CREDIT CARDS MC, V
CHILDREN accepted
DISABLED one ground-floor bedroom
PETS small dogs accepted
CLOSED never
LANGUAGES English, French
PROPRIETOR Rosanna Battistelli

PERUGIA

ASSISI

UMBRA
~ TOWN HOTEL ~

Via degli Archi 6, Assisi, 06081 Perugia
TEL (075) 812240 **FAX** (075) 813653 **E-MAIL** humbra@mail.caribusiness.it
WEBSITE www.caribusiness.it/carifo/az/hotelumbra

IN A CITY NOT NOTED FOR quality small-scale hotels, the delightful family-run Umbra cannot be ignored. Tucked away down a little alley off the main square, the Umbra consists of several little houses – some of which date back to the 13thC – with a small gravelled courtyard garden shaded by a pergola. The interior is comfortable, and in parts more like a private home than a hotel: there is a bright little sitting-room with Mediterranean-style tiles and brocaded wing armchairs and a series of bedrooms, mostly quite simply furnished, but each with its own character. When we returned to reconsider the hotel for this guide, we enjoyed eating in the elegant dining-room but agreed with past reports that the food was only 'all right'. Happily, there is no shortage of nearby alternative eating places.

The Umbra offers all the peace and quiet which you might hope to find in Assisi, and nothing is too much trouble for Alberto Laudenzi, whose family has run the hotel for more than 50 years. We think that it is the best middle-range accommodation Perugia can offer. However, one reader reports that some of the bedrooms need redecoration, and another that parking can be a problem.

~

NEARBY Basilica of St Francis and other main sights.
LOCATION in the middle of Assisi, off Piazza del Comune, with a small garden; nearest car park some distance away
FOOD breakfast, lunch, dinner
PRICE €€
ROOMS 20 double, 5 single, all with bath; all rooms have phone, central heating, TV; most have air-conditioning
FACILITIES 3 sitting-rooms, bar, dining-room **CREDIT CARDS**redit cards AE, DC, MC, V
CHILDREN tolerated **DISABLED** access difficult
PETS not accepted
CLOSED mid-Jan to mid-Mar
PROPRIETOR Alberto Laudenzi

PERUGIA

BOVARA DI TREVI

CASA GIULIA
~ COUNTRY VILLA ~

Via Corciano 1, Bovara di Trevi, 06039 Perugia
TEL (0742) 78257 **FAX** (0742) 381632
E-MAIL casagiulia@umbria.net **WEBSITE** www.casagiulia.com

CASA GIULIA, parts of which go back to the 14thC, is both an excellent base for touring Umbria's famous cities (Assisi, Perugia, Spoleto and Todi are all within easy driving distance) and a great place in which to relax from the rigours of cultural tourism. Con-venient for the main Spoleto-Perugia highway, but in no way disturbed by traffic, the villa has a withdrawn character as though time stopped still here sometime in the 1930s. The principal sitting-room (open only on request), is a long rectangular area with doors and windows opening on to the garden, and is full of bric-a-brac collected by the owner's grandparents: objets d'art, old toys and cameras displayed in a glass-fronted bookcase, a collection of antique walking-sticks and umbrellas.

In the rest of the house a solid, bourgeois atmosphere reigns. The breakfast-room is elegant and uncluttered, with a black-and-white marble tiled floor (in summer breakfast is served under a pergola, just in front of the house). Bedrooms are a touch spartan, perhaps because some of them are located in the old servants' quarters – more a question of atmosphere than comfort.

~

NEARBY Assisi (22 km); Perugia (50 km); Spoleto (12 km).
LOCATION in its own grounds just outside village of Bovara, near Trevi; own car parking
FOOD breakfast
PRICE €€
ROOMS 7 doubles: 5 with own bath or shower; 2 sharing one bathroom; 2 mini-apartments for 3 people (min. stay 3 days) with kitchenettes
FACILITIES sitting-room, breakfast-room, garden, swimming-pool, meeting-room
CREDIT CARDS accepted
CHILDREN welcome
DISABLED one suitableroom **PETS** please check first
CLOSED never **LANGUAGES** French, some English
PROPRIETOR Caterina Alessandrini Petrucci

PERUGIA

CAMPELLO SUL CLITUNNO

IL VECCHIO MOLINO
~ OLD MILL ~

Loc.Pissignano, Via del Tempio 34, 06042 Perugia
TEL (0743) 521122 **FAX** (0743) 275097
WEBSITE www.perugiaonline.com

IT IS A MYSTERY how this inn, so close to the busy Perugia-Spoleto road, remains such an oasis of tranquillity. Almost the only sound is of gurgling brooks winding through the leafy gardens. As befits an old mill, all the buildings live in close harmony with the river: the drive sweeps around the mill pond to a creeper-covered building against which big old grinding-stones rest. The gardens are a spit of land, with weeping willows dipping into streams on both sides. Water even runs through some of the old working parts, where the mill machinery has been built into the decorative scheme.

There seems to be no end to the number of public rooms, all furnished in a highly individual manner: elegant white couches in front of a big brick fireplace, surmounted by carved wooden lamps; tables with lecterns bearing early editions of Dante's Purgatorio; mill wheels used as doors. The bedrooms were, we were relieved to note, pleasingly dry and decorated in a restrained manner with fine antiques, the white walls lit up by parchment-shaded lamps.

Remember that the hotel is popular in the wedding season and during the Spoleto festival.

~

NEARBY Spoleto (11 km); Perugia (50 km).
LOCATION 50 km SE of Perugia between Trevi and Spoleto; in its own grounds by the Clitunno river; ample car parking
FOOD breakfast
PRICE ⓔ-ⓔⓔ
ROOMS 2 single, 6 double, 5 suites, all with bath or shower, phone, minibar; some with air-conditioning Facilities sitting-rooms, bar, gardens
SMOKING permitted **CREDIT CARDS** AE, DC, EC, MC, V
CHILDREN welcome **DISABLED** access difficult **PETS** small dogs accepted
CLOSED Nov-Mar **LANGUAGES** English, French, German
PROPRIETOr Paolo Rapanelli

PERUGIA

CANALICCHIO

RELAIS IL CANALICCHIO
~ HILLTOP HOTEL ~

Via della Piazza 13, 06050 Canalicchio, Perugia
TEL (075) 8707325 **FAX** (075) 8707296
E-MAIL relais@ntt.it **WEBSITE** www.wel.it/Rcanalicchio.html

ONE OF THE PARADOXES of modern Italy is that what were once the modest homes of farmers and artisans have become, with careful restoration, exemplars of modern taste and comfort. What makes this possible is the Italian genius for combining everyday materials of quality – brick, wood, plaster, terracotta – with style and flair.

The owners of Relais Il Canalicchio have taken over most of the semi-fortified, hilltop town of the same name and created a hotel that not only respects the native Umbrian qualities but imaginatively enhances them with contemporary Italian panache. Public rooms are in the old working areas of the mill: brick arches and the massive grinding-stones set off the comfortable, elegant furniture. The plain plaster walls are decorated with English prints, oil portraits and brilliant local ceramics. An old wine-press remains.

Each bedroom has been individually furnished; some have terrace gardens and many have superb views. The restaurant serves exquisitely prepared produce from its own farm. If you feel guilty about such hedonism, there is a gym, a pool and a sauna. Even if you are a prince, this is one hamlet certainly good enough for you.
~

NEARBY Perugia, Assisi, Gubbio, Todi (all within 40 km).
LOCATION quiet hill-top village 40 km SE of Perugia
FOOD breakfast, lunch, dinner
PRICE €€-€€€€
ROOMS 18 double; 5 single; 4 suites; all with bath or shower, TV, air-conditioning, minibar, safe
FACILITIES sitting-rooms, restaurant, billiard-roomswimming-pool, gym, sauna, mountain bikes; terraces, gardens Smoking permitted
CREDIT CARDS AE, DC, MC, V **CHILDREN** welcome
DISABLED some rooms suitable **PETS** small dogs
CLOSED never **LANGUAGES** English, French, German
PROPRIETOR Antonio Setter

PERUGIA

CASALINI

LA ROSA CANINA
~ FARM GUEST-HOUSE ~

Via dei Mandorli 23, Loc. Casalini, Panicale, 06064 Perugia
TEL & FAX (075) 8350660
E-MAIL info@larosacanina.it **WEBSITE** www.larosacanina.it

A LONG AND WINDING TRACK takes you out of the village of Casalini for
almost 3 km before you reach the hushed, olive-flanked valley where
La Rosa Canina lies. Sandro Belardinelli and his wife made their home
here in 1989, setting aside part of two 15thC cottages as guest quarters.

The dog-rose, from which the farm takes its name, is just one of the profusion of flowers which give the banks of the front garden their perennial
colour. Behind the house, the menagerie of animals and the wire-fenced
vegetable garden breathe real country living into what might have been
just another converted farmhouse.

Inside, the guest rooms are reasonably proportioned and furnished with
a hotch-potch of furniture, old and not so old. The wooden mangers in the
downstairs dining-room are a reminder that it was once a cattle stall. The
dinner menu, based upon traditional cucina umbra, varies according to
season, but Swiss-born Signora Belardinelli places emphasis on the quality
of her food – all vegetables are home produce, as is the olive oil, much of
the meat, and the jam on the breakfast table

~

NEARBY Lake Trasimeno (8 km); Panicale (8 km).
LOCATION 3 km along a track, above the village of Casalini, ample car parking
FOOD breakfast and dinner
PRICE B&B €; minimum stay 3 nights
ROOMS 5 double and 3 triple rooms, all with bath; all rooms centrally heated.
FACILITIES restaurant; garden, swimming-pool, riding (lessons also available),
archery, table-tennis, bowls
CREDIT CARDS AE, EC, MC, V
CHILDREN accepted
DISABLED no special facilities
PETS not accepted
CLOSED Nov to Easter.
LANGUAGES German, some English
PROPRIETOR Sandro Belardinelli

PERUGIA

CASTEL RIGONE

RELAIS LA FATTORIA
~ TOWN HOTEL ~

Via Rigone 1, Castel Rigone, Lago Trasimeno, 06060 Perugia
TEL (075) 845322 **FAX** (075) 845197
E-MAIL pammelati@edisons.it **WEBSITE** www.relaislafattoria.com

ON THE HILLS behind Lake Trasimeno lies the small medieval town of Castel Rigone, a mere handful of houses grouped about a handsome piazza, and right at its centre is this pleasant, family-run hotel occupying what was once a manor house.

You feel a sense of welcome the moment you step inside the reception, with its wooden ceiling, stone walls and comfortable Knole sofas; keen young staff are on hand. The public rooms are tastefully decorated, with Persian rugs on the polished cork floors and bright modern paintings on the white walls. The only addition to the building that has been allowed by the Italian Fine Arts Ministry is a restaurant perfectly in keeping with the original style. Dishes include fresh fish from the lake. Bed-rooms have been designed with an eye more to modern comfort than to individual style and some have lake views. The bathrooms are bright and new.

Along the entire front of the house is a terrace with sitting areas and a small swimming-pool. An extensive buffet breakfast (home-made bread and jams, cheeses and cured meats) is served here in fine weather.

~

NEARBY Perugia (27 km); Assisi (35 km); Gubbio (50 km).
LOCATION 27 km NW of Perugia, in centre of town; car parking nearby
FOOD breakfast, lunch, dinner
PRICE €-€€€€
ROOMS 3 single, 23 double, 3 junior suites, all with bath or shower (suites with Jacuzzis); phone, TV, minibar
FACILITIES sitting-room, restaurant, terrace/garden, swimming-pool
CREDIT CARDS AE, DC, EC, MC, V **CHILDREN** welcome
DISABLED no special facilities
PETS check first **CLOSED** never; restaurant only, Jan **LANGUAGES** English, French, German
PROPRIETORS Pammelati family

PERUGIA

CENERENTE

CASTELLO DELL'OSCANO
~ CONVERTED CASTLE ~

Loc. Cenerente, 06134 Perugia
TEL (075) 690 125 **FAX** (075) 690 666
E-MAIL info@oscano.com **WEBSITE** www.oscano.it

A T FIRST SIGHT Castello dell'Oscáno appears like a fairytale medieval castle: ivy-clad turrets, battlements and crenellated towers rise above a steep, hillside pine forest. In fact, this is an 18thC re-creation, and the inside reveals the 18thC's genius for civilized living.

The interiors are finely proportioned, spacious and light. The hall rises the entire height of the castle, with an imposing carved stairway, polished wood floors and neo-Gothic windows. One public room leads into another, all filled with the castle's original furniture: a library which will entrance any bibliophile with its carved Classical book-cases and 18thC volumes; sitting-rooms with wooden panelling, tapestries and sculpted fireplaces; a dining-room with old display cases full of Deruta pottery.

Upstairs, the floors are of geometrically patterned, black-and-white marble. There are only ten bedrooms in the castle, each with its own antique furnishing. The remainder, in the Villa Ada next door, are less exciting and cheaper. The most spectacular (but strictly for the agile) is in the turret, with a four-poster bed and a door to the ramparts which look over the romantic gardens below.

~

NEARBY Perugia (5 km); Assisi (28 km); Gubbio (40 km).
LOCATION on a hillside in its own grounds; ample car parking
FOOD breakfast, dinner
PRICE €€€€ (Castello)–€€ (Villa Ada)
ROOMS 11 double (Castello), 8 double, 2 single (Villa Ada); all with bath or shower, phone, TV, minibar, air-conditioning
FACILITIES bar, gardens, swimming-pool
CREDIT CARDS AE, DC, EC, MC, V **CHILDREN** welcome
DISABLED 1 suitable bedroom
PETS accepted
CLOSED never; restaurant only, 15 Jan to 15 Feb
LANGUAGES English, French
MANAGER Maurizio Bussolati

PERUGIA

FOLIGNO

VILLA RONCALLI
~ TOWN VILLA ~

Via Roma 25, Foligno, 06034 Perugia
TEL (0742) 391091 **FAX** (0742) 391001

DON'T BE PUT OFF by the depressing light-industrial surroundings in which this splendid 18thC villa now finds itself. The tall chestnut trees which line the drive and encircle this former hunting lodge screen off the outside world almost entirely.

Although the present owners acquired the villa only relatively recently, they have succeeded in creating within it the atmosphere of a family home. The public rooms are furnished with magnificent pieces of antique furniture and paintings.

The ground floor is dominated by the elegant dining-room, formerly the villa's entrance hall, with its long sideboard and massive glass-fronted wine cabinet. Angelo's wife Alessandra runs the kitchen, which has become one of the gastronomic temples of central Umbria, while their daughter Maria Luisa oversees the front-of-house with amiable efficiency.

Upstairs, on the piano nobile, four airy bedrooms with large shuttered windows lead off the cool, frescoed sitting-room, while the remainder are in the mansarded second floor. Each is furnished opulently in a timeless modern style.

~

NEARBY Spello (7 km); Montefalco (12 km); Assisi (15 km).
LOCATION 1.5 km S of Foligno; ample parking
FOOD breakfast, lunch, dinner
PRICE rooms (€); DB&B (€)(€)(€)
ROOMS 8 double, 2 singles with shower, air-conditioning, television, minibar, heating
FACILITIES sitting-room, breakfast room, restaurant, bar
CREDIT CARDS DC, AE, V, MC
CHILDREN accepted
DISABLED no facilities **PETS** not accepted **CLOSED** restaurant only, 4 to 20 Mar
LANGUAGES English, French
PROPRIETORS Angelo and Alessandra Scolastra

PERUGIA

VILLA MONTEGRANELLI
∿ COUNTRY VILLA ∿

Loc. Monteluiano, Gubbio, 06024 Perugia
TEL (075) 9220185 **FAX** (075) 9273372
E-MAIL montegra@tin.it **WEBSITE** www.italyintour.com/ umbria/montegranelli

THE FACT THAT THIS 18thC villa is based on an original fortified building of the 13thC helps to explain the unadorned severity of the exterior. Massive and square, built of hewn stone, it stands in its own park surrounded by pines and centuries-old cypresses. From the gardens there is a view over to the light-grey stone city hanging on to the mountainside (a view that unfortunately includes the cement factory that has been allowed next to this dignified town).

In stark contrast, most of the interiors are in a light 18thC style: airily spacious public rooms with ornate plasterwork, frescoes and elaborate marble door surrounds, probably more suitable for the numerous weddings and official functions that take place here than for sitting and relaxing. The bedrooms are much more simply done (except for the main suite) and some are quite small. They all have excellent bathrooms.

The breakfast- and dining-rooms are in the lower, 13thC, part of the villa, with thick stone walls, vaulted ceilings and old brick arches. It is renowned for its restaurant, and you will appreciate the sophisticated cuisine and attentive service.

∿

NEARBY Gubbio (5 km); Perugia (38 km); Assisi (35 km).
LOCATION 5 km SW of Gubbio, in its own grounds; ample car parking
FOOD breakfast,lunch, dinner
PRICE €€-€€€
ROOMS 20 double, 1 single, all with bath or shower, phone, TV, minibar
FACILITIES sitting-rooms, restaurant, gardens
CREDIT CARDS AE, DC, EC, MC, V **CHILDREN** welcome
DISABLED no special facilities
PETS dogs accepted
CLOSED never
LANGUAGES English, French, German
PROPRIETOR Salvatore Mongelli

PERUGIA

FATTORIA DI VIBIO
~ FARM GUEST-HOUSE ~

Loc. Buchella 1a, 9-Doglio, Montescastello Vibio, 05010 Perugia
TEL (075) 8749607 **FAX** (075) 8780014
E-MAIL info@fattoriadivibio.com **WEBSITE** www.fattoriadivibio.com

OCCASIONALLY, the whole atmosphere of a place is captured by a small detail: here it is the hand-painted pottery used to serve Signora Saladini's delicious meals which reveals the relaxed elegance of this renovated 18thC farmhouse. The style is modern rustic Italian, with pleasing open spaces, defined by white walls that contrast with the colourful fabrics and ceramics. Light, airy and well-proportioned, there is an air of effortless simplicity which, you quickly realize, required a great deal of taste and effort. Most of the bedrooms, of similar style, are in the house next door.

The Saladini family are serious about their visitors' comforts and well-being (but we've had a disappointed reader's letter since the last edition). Much of what is offered in the dining-room comes out of the farm or the market garden and the preparation is a spectacle in itself, open to all. The mandatory half-board should not prove a penance. If you need to lose calories, you can swim, play table-tennis, ride or walk in the magnificent countryside around; tennis is also available nearby. Or you may prefer to relax in the quiet of the garden. Otherwise, there is not much to do – but then that is the whole point of this soothing guest-house.

~

NEARBY Todi (20 km); Orvieto (30 km).
LOCATION on quiet hillside off S448 road between Todi and Orvieto; ample car parking
FOOD breakfast, lunch, dinner
PRICE €€€-€€€ (half-board); one week minimum stay in August
ROOMS 10 double, all with bath or shower; some with TV
FACILITIES sitting-room, dining-room and terrace, garden, swimming-pool, bikes, horse-riding, fishing
SMOKING permitted **CREDIT CARDS** AE, EC, DC, MC, V **CHILDREN** welcome
DISABLED one suitable room **PETS** small dogs **CLOSED** Jan and Feb, Nov to Dec
LANGUAGES French, little English
PROPRIETORS Gabriella, Giuseppe & Filippo Saladini

PERUGIA

MONTEFALCO

VILLA PAMBUFFETTI
~ VILLA HOTEL ~

Via della Vittoria 20, Montefalco 06036 Perugia
TEL (0742) 379417, 378823 **FAX** (0742) 379245
E-MAIL villabianca@interbusiness.it **WEBSITE** www.umbria.org

LIKE HEMINGWAY IN SPAIN, the poet D'Annunzio seems to have stayed everywhere in Italy; however, in the case of Villa Pambuffetti the claim is better justified than most. Not only did he dedicate a poem to the nearby walled town of Montefalco (known as 'Um-bria's balcony' for its unrivalled views of the region, but the villa itself has a turn-of-the-century elegance that fits the poet's legend.

Ten thousand square metres of shady garden surround the main building. Inside, furniture and decoration have been kept almost as they were at the start of the 1900s when the Pambuffetti family began taking 'paying guests': floors and panelling of seasoned oak, bamboo armchairs (which took D'Annunzio's fancy), Tiffany lampshades and old family photographs in art nouveau frames pay tribute to a century that started optimistically. Many of the bedrooms are furnished with the family's older and finer antiques and all have bathrooms which, though recent, are, stylistically, nearly perfect. If you like a room with a view, try the tower, which has one of the six-windowed, all-round variety. The dining-room's view is more modest, but then the food deserves attention, too.

~

NEARBY Montefalco, Assisi (30 km); Perugia (46 km).
LOCATION just outside Montefalco, in its own grounds; ample car parking
FOOD breakfast, dinner
PRICE €€€-€€€€
ROOMS 11 double; 1 single; 3 suites; 2 with bath, the rest with shower, TV, minibar, air-conditioning
FACILITIES sitting-room, bar restaurant, loggia, garden, swimming-pool
CREDIT CARDS AE, DC, MC, V
CHILDREN welcome
DISABLED 2 rooms on ground floor **PETS** not accepted
CLOSED never
LANGUAGES English, French, German, Spanish
MANAGERS Alessandra and Mauro Angelucci

PERUGIA

LE GROTTE DI BOLDRINO
~ TOWN HOTEL ~

Via Virgilio Cappari 30, Panicale, 06064 Perugia
TEL (075) 837161 **FAX** (075) 837166

THE FORMER PALAZZO Belleschi-Grifoni, hewn into the walls of the medieval brick-built hill town of Panicale, was converted only in 1990 to its present use. In contrast to its stern front, the interior is small and intimate, designed in the finest contemporary manner, with particularly imaginative use of iron and wood.

The hotel can be entered through a doorway from one of the narrow passageways of the old borgo or, more conveniently, via the lower restaurant entrance on the road which encircles the town. A warren-like corridor takes you to the parquet-floored bedrooms. In surprising contrast to their modern finish, they are furnished with imperious late-19thC furniture – towering walnut bedheads, and so on. Noteworthy also is the gentle use of lighting.

The reputation of the downstairs restaurant is increasing by leaps and bounds. Again, you find a pleasing juxtaposition of old and new, with the unplastered medieval wall and traditional oak and brick-tile ceiling against the modern plastered walls and iron railings of the restaurant's upper gallery. The short, mainly Umbrian, menu offers a variety of local specialities.

~

NEARBY Castiglione del Lago (15 km); Città della Pieve (25 km).
LOCATION built into the town walls, parking nearby
FOOD breakfast, lunch and dinner
PRICE rooms (€); restaurant (€)(€)
ROOMS 9 double rooms, 2 singles, all with bath or shower, TV, telephone
FACILITIES restaurant, breakfast room, sitting-room
CREDIT CARDS AE, DC, MC, V
CHILDREN accepted **DISABLED** access difficult
PETS small pets accepted
CLOSED never
LANGUAGES French, some English
PROPRIETOR Attilio Spadoni

PERUGIA

PANICALE

VILLA DI MONTESOLARE
~ COUNTRY VILLA HOTEL ~

Loc. Colle San Paolo, Panicale, 06070 Perugia
TEL *(075) 832376* **FAX** *(075) 8355462*
E-MAIL info@villamontesolare.it **WEBSITE** www.villamontesolare.it

HIGH WALLS KEEP OUT the arid scenery around, enclosing the stuccoed villa in a green oasis. The present building dates back to 1780, although the 16thC chapel in the garden suggests a much earlier house was on the site. When the present owners bought it, they set about restoring the 19thC garden (and the secret garden behind it), building the swimming-pool a discreet distance away, and converting the villa without interfering with its patrician character.

The result is one of the most comfortable country retreats of the Trasimeno area. The bedrooms of the villa retain their original character – beamed ceilings, quarry tile floors and whitewashed walls, furnished in squirely fashion with turn-of-the-century high- backed beds, cabinets and wardrobes. The cool blue sitting-room on the piano nobile certainly is noble, while the dining-rooms and the bar are situated more humbly, downstairs In 1995, Mrs Strunk and her husband Filippo converted a casa colonica which stands outside the walls. They divided it into five suites, building by it the villa's second swimming-pool. Another annexe has also been added recently. Rooms are simply furnished in country style.

~

NEARBY Panicale (12 km); Città della Pieve (25 km).
LOCATION 2 km N of the SS 220, direction Colle S. Paolo; ample car parking
FOOD breakfast, lunch and dinner
PRICE DB&B€€€-€€€; minimum stay three days
ROOMS 8 double with bathroom; two suites in the villa; 10 suites in 2 annexes
FACILITIES 2 dining-rooms, bar, sitting-room; 2 swimming-pools, tennis court, bowls, riding
CREDIT CARDS DC, MC, V **CHILDREN** accepted
DISABLED 1 suitable apartment **PETS** if small, well-behaved **CLOSEDI** 18 Dec to 10 Jan
LANGUAGES English, German, French
PROPRIETOR Rosemarie Strunk

PERUGIA

PONTE PATTOLI

IL COVONE
∼ COUNTRY VILLA GUEST-HOUSE ∼

Strada della Fratticiola 2, Ponte Pattoli, 06080 Perugia
TEL (075) 694140 **FAX** (075) 694503
E-MAIL covone@mercurio.it **WEBSITE** www.italiaabc.com

Parts of Villa Il Covone date back to medieval times – the tower was once used to watch over the nearby Tiber. Today, the visitor is more conscious of the 18thC additions and the romantically peeling 19thC façade, which gives it the air of a classic Italianate villa.

The main hall, once an open courtyard, now glassed over, and the downstairs sitting-rooms hold the family accretions of several centuries – portraits hanging higgledy-piggledy on cracking plaster remind you that this is still the Taticchi family's home. Upstairs, the guest quarters comprise bedrooms of different shapes and sizes, each spacious and high-ceilinged. The furniture has certainly seen better days (as has the house), but that is exactly what gives the place its charm. The eight rooms in the annex, across the way in the equestrian centre, are more modern, and perhaps more comfortable, but lack the fading splendour of the main house.

Dinner, shared with the family around one large table, includes Umbrian specialities such as gnocchetti di ricotta (small potato dumplings in a ricotta cheese sauce), pork roasted in the wood oven and gelato in cialda (ice cream in a nest of sponge).

∼

NEARBY Perugia (10 km); Assisi (30 km).
LOCATION 2 km W of SS3-bis; gardens and private car parking
FOOD breakfast, lunch and evening meal
PRICE rooms ⓔ; DB&B ⓔ-ⓔⓔ
ROOMS 4 double rooms in villa, not all with private bathroom; 8 double rooms with shower, in annex
FACILITIES sitting room, dining-room; billiards, table-tennis; garden, horse-riding (lessons available)
CREDIT CARDS AE, MC, V
CHILDREN accepted
DISABLED no facilities available **PETS** small animals only
CLOSED never **LANGUAGES** Some English
PROPRIETORS Cesare and Elena Taticchi

PERUGIA

SCRITTO

SEMI DI MELA
～ FARMHOUSE HOTEL ～

Loc. Petroia 36, Scritto, Gubbio, 06020 Perugia
TEL & FAX (075) 920039
WEBSITE www. gubbio.perlenelverde.it

A DIFFICULT TRACK takes you down, past the castle of Petroia, to this *casa colonica*, a farm worker's cottage restored over a decade ago. A downstairs beam shows that it was already standing in 1690, but its recent restoration has rather deprived it of that rough, rural character. The traditional oak and brick ceilings remain, but the smooth plasterwork and neat carpentry are all too perfect.

The bedrooms are comfortable, furnished simply in traditional rustic style. Every window opens on to awesome views of the Appennine mountains to the east of Gubbio.

Francesco Pellegrini grows organic food for the supper table on his ten acres of land, as well as olives and cereal crops, while Antonella tends the poultry which roam freely around the yard, and runs the kitchen. The emphasis of the evenings is that very Italian pursuit of *stare insieme* (getting together). Individual tables in the dining-room have recently been replaced with a single large one at which Antonella and Francesco eat with their guests. Their limited knowledge of English or other languages is made up for by the warmth of their hospitality.

～

NEARBY Gubbio (15 km); Perugia (25 km).
LOCATION 2 km E of the SS298 between Perugia and Gubbio
FOOD breakfast and dinner
PRICE rooms €; DB&B €€; minimum stay two days, one week in August
ROOMS 5 double rooms (1 for four people) with shower
FACILITIES sitting/dining- room; terrace, garden, archery, mountain bikes
CREDIT CARDS not accepted
CHILDREN accepted
DISABLED no special facilities
PETS not accepted
CLOSED 6 Jan to early Mar
LANGUAGES some English
PROPRIETORS Antonella Requale & Francesco Pellegrini

PERUGIA

SPOLETO

GATTAPONE
Town hotel

Via del Ponte 6, Spoleto, 06049 Perugia
Tel (0743) 223447 **Fax** (0743) 223448
E-mail gattapone@mail.caribusiness.it **Website** www.caribusiness.it/gattapone

There are two things you can do in this hotel just outside Spoleto's centre. The most obvious is to gape at the unparalleled views of the 13thC Bridge of Towers spanning the Tessino Valley. The other is to enjoy the quaintness of its Sixties jet-set decoration, all wood, glass, chrome and leather. If you tire, as some do, of the rustic antique look, then you will enjoy the now dated, but meticulously maintained 'modern' style.

The hotel is a favourite of the Festival crowd, and the walls of the bar are festooned with pictures of the famous and would-be famous who throng its salons late into the evening. Even if you do not stay at the Gattapone, you will notice it. From the outside it looks like a solid, two-storey villa with classic ochre walls and green shutters. Inside, one notices how the original building and its more modern extension have been constructed downwards to exploit the hillside position. Many of the bedrooms have large picture windows to capture the panorama.

We visited the hotel in low season and enjoyed the peace and quiet. During the Festival (June-July), rooms are hard to get.

Nearby Assisi 48 km; Todi 42 km; Perugia 63 km.
Location on hillside, just outside historic centre of Spoleto; no special parking facilities
Food breakfast
Price €€€-€€€€€
Rooms 7 double, 7 junior suites, all with bath or shower, phone, TV, minibar
Facilities breakfast-room, sitting-room, bar, terrace
Credit cards AE, DC, EC, MC, V
Children welcome
Disabled no special facilities
Pets accepted
Closed never
Languages English, French
Proprietor Pier Giulio Hanke

PERUGIA

SPOLETO

LA MACCHIA
~ COUNTRY HOTEL ~

Loc. Licina 11, Spoleto 06049 Perugia
TEL & FAX (0743) 49059

SPOLETO, ONE OF THE MOST interesting of the southern Umbrian towns, is also one of the most congested, with a confusing one-way system and few places to park. From late June until mid-July, during Spoleto's world-famous Festival of Two Worlds, it is also notoriously difficult to find a room. This quiet hotel, tucked away in the fold of a hillside, yet close to the centre, offers a welcome alternative for those in search of a peaceful stay.

Carla and Claudio's hotel started life in the 1980s as a country osteria specializing in the local *cucina spoletana*. It was only recently that they opened their hotel. A separate entrance spares guests from the occasional inconvenience caused by large dinners in the downstairs banqueting room. The style throughout is modern, though the old barn, now a shady portico, and the gnarled olive tree in the front courtyard, are a reminder of the building's original use.

In each of the well-lit bedrooms, the chestnut furniture has been made by local craftsmen. Some beds have old wrought-iron heads and splendidly firm bases.

~

NEARBY Spoleto (2 km); Fonti di Clitunno (10 km).
LOCATION 0.5 km from the old via Flaminia, just N of Spoleto; ample car parking
FOOD breakfast, lunch, dinner
PRICE rooms € with breakfast
ROOMS 10 double, 1 single with shower, air-conditioning, satellite television, minibar, central heating
FACILITIES sitting-room, breakfast room, bar, restaurant, garden
CREDIT CARDS AE, DC, MC, V
CHILDREN accepted
DISABLED 2 bedrooms
PETS not accepted
CLOSED never; restaurant only, Tue
LANGUAGES English
PROPRIETORS Carla Marini and Claudio Sabatini

PERUGIA

SPOLETO

SAN LUCA
∼ TOWN HOTEL ∼

Via Interna delle Mura 21, Spoleto 06049, Perugia
TEL (0743) 223399 **FAX** (0743) 223800

W HEN POPE INNOCENT II came to this spot in 1198, his holy presence is reputed to have caused a fountain miraculously to begin spouting clear and plentiful water, thus giving immediate relief and renewed strength to himself and his retinue. Today the site is occupied by an impressive 19thC building with soft yellow painted walls, wooden doors and shutters, and a red-tiled roof, which was transformed after extensive renovation into an elegant hotel in 1995. The yellow colour scheme continues inside in the light, sunny hallway and sitting areas, where comfortable armchairs, some upholstered in bright yellow, others, more modern, in black leather, blend stylishly with antique furniture, a display of china tureens and attractive arrangements of flowers and plants. Several of the pastel-toned bedrooms have a balcony or terrace; all of them are sound-proofed and have large bathrooms with telephones.

Right in the centre of Spoleto, but peacefully set in lush gardens, the San Luca also has a roof garden as well as a spacious internal courtyard, where it is still possible to sample the 'therapeutic' properties of the waters. We would welcome more reports.

∼

NEARBY Assisi 48 km; Todi 42 km.
LOCATION in historic city centre; car parking
FOOD buffet breakfast
PRICE €€€-€€€€€
ROOMS 32 double, 3 single, 1 suite, all with bath (some with Jacuzzi), 5 with shower, phone, air-conditioning, minibar, hairdrier, safe
FACILITIES 2 sitting-rooms, breakfast-room, conference room, 2 lifts, courtyard, garden, roof garden
CREDIT CARDS AE, DC, MC, V
CHILDREN welcome **DISABLED** two adapted rooms **PETS** smalll dogs accepted
CLOSED never **LANGUAGES** English, German, French
PROPRIETOR Daniela Zuccari

PERUGIA

TODI

SAN VALENTINO
~ CONVERTED MONASTERY ~

Loc. San Valentino, Todi, 06059 Perugia
TEL (075) 8944103,

WHEN FIRST VISITED San Valentino, we sensed that a slightly quirky atmosphere reigned in this former monastery, as if the buildings themselves had not fully accepted their conversion to the needs of a luxury hotel. At least, this was our impression, sitting in the former church which served as the social hub of the complex.

That was for the first edition of the guide. As we go to press for this new edition the hotel is closed for a major renovation programme, and it is impossibe to establish when it will reopen. Nonetheless, we're retaining the entry, because this is an interesting address, with great potential.

We hope that the lovely 13thC Umbrian fresco of the Crucifixion is still in place. Where the altar might have been there was a bar and below, in the crypt, a piano to encourage late-night crooners to join in with My Way rather than Dies Irae. The remainder of the hotel, more conventional in decoration and atmosphere, fully exploited its prime position looking over to the gracious silhouette of nearby Todi.

Reports welcome.

~

NEARBY Todi (4 km); Perugia (35 km); Orvieto (35 km).
LOCATION in its own grounds,on hillside outside Todi;ample car parking
FOOD breakfast, snacks
PRICE €€€-€€€€€
ROOMS 4 double, 1 single, 3 suites, all with bath or shower
FACILITIES breakfast-room,sitting-room, bar, garden,swimming-pool, tennis
CREDIT CARDS AE, MC, DC, V
CHILDREN please check first
DISABLED not suitable
PETS small dogs accepted
CLOSED variable
LANGUAGES French, Spanish,some English
PROPRIETOR Sig. Baresi

PERUGIA

TORGIANO

LE TRE VASELLE
⌁ TOWN HOTEL ⌁

Via Garibaldi 48, Torgiano, 06089 Perugia
TEL (075) 9880447 **FAX** (075) 9880214
E-MAIL 3vaselle@3vaselle.it **WEBSITE** www.3vaselle.it

THREE MONASTIC WINE JUGS discovered during the restoration of the original 17thC palazzo are what give this exceptional hotel its name and its theme: wine. Owned by the Lungarotti family, makers of Umbria's finest vintages, the palazzo is packed with still lifes of grapes, prints of the gods carousing and statues of Bacchus. However, nothing but sober professionalism characterizes the day-to-day management.

Bedrooms, some in a more modern building behind the main one and others in a luxury annexe a short walk away, are all furnished to the highest standards: comfortable striped sofas, antique chests, individually chosen prints and lamps give an air of unrushed elegance. Public rooms are open and spacious, spanned by sweeping white arches and softly lit. Breakfast, an extensive buffet, is served on a secluded back terrace. The restaurant is outstanding, with a wine-list the size of a telephone directory.

A recent visitor to Le Tre Vaselle could report only improvements. It could not be more professional; you could not feel more at home.

⌁

NEARBY Deruta (5 km); Perugia (8 km); Assisi (16 km).
LOCATION in quiet street of village of Torgiano, 13 km SE of Perugia; car parking in nearby piazza
FOOD breakfast, lunch, dinner
PRICE €€€€-€€€€€
ROOMS 52 double, 2 singles, 7 suites; most with bath, some with shower; all rooms have central heating, air-conditioning, phone, TV
FACILITIES sitting-rooms, dining-rooms, breakfast-room, bar, terrace, swimming-pool, sauna
CREDIT CARDS AE, DC, MC, V
CHILDREN welcome **DISABLED** access possible
PETS not accepted
CLOSED never
LANGUAGES English, French, German
MANAGER Giovanni Margheritini

PERUGIA

UMBERTIDE

BORGO SAN BIAGIO
～ SELF CATERING HAMLET ～

Bookings only through CV Travel in the U.K.
TEL *(00 44) 020 7591 2811* **FAX** *(00 44) 020 7591 2802*
E-MAIL *in@cvtravel.net* **WEBSITE** *www.cvrtravel.net*

A T NOON AND 6 PM the chapel bell tolls, as it has for hundreds of years, over this isolated hamlet on top of an Umbrian hill. Once a medieval community, now it consists of seven dwellings, rescued from ruin and individually equipped, plus a communal living/dining area and a large communal living area/games room in the old chapel. It's one of the most enchanting self-catering operations we've seen in Italy. We're reluctant to include such places unless they offer a certain level of service; here, not only the bell is rung, but the beds are changed (with cotton sheets) and dinner will be cooked each night if you want. The owner, friendly Renato Rondina, began restoring it in the early 1990s, bringing it off with skill and high standards: comfortable beds, cooking facilities and CD players in each dwelling. It's ideal for a group to rent together because taking just one of the houses, and having to rub along with unknown neighbours, might spoil the very special intimacy and peace. There's a great sense of timelessness, space, views to keep you musing for hours and an extra-long swimming pool. Crowning all is a 1,000-year-old, remarkably restored tower, sleeping two. The photo was taken from its roof, on which is a second (miniature) swimming pool.

～

NEARBY Cortona, Umbertide, Sansepolcro, Monterchi.
LOCATION very isolated, on hill top in own grounds – directions essential, supplied on booking
FOOD self-catering, but dinner by arrangement; real pizza oven
PRICE middle-range self-catering
ROOMS 7 self-catering dwellings, sleeping 2-4, all with en suite showers, living rooms, central heating, some with phone
FACILITIES games room, garden, swimming-pool
CREDIT CARDS prepayment required, AE, MC, V accepted
CHILDREN accepted **DISABLED** unsuitable **PETS** not accepted
CLOSED never **LANGUAGES** English
PROPRIETOR Renato Rondina

TERNI

BASCHI

POMURLO VECCHIO/LE CASETTE
~ COUNTRY GUEST-HOUSES ~

Loc. Pomurlo Vecchio, Baschi, 05023 Terni
TEL (0744) 950190/950475 **FAX** (0744) 950500

LAZZARO MINGHELLI's 350-acre farm estate stretches from the southern shores of Lago di Corbara almost as far as Baschi. His romantic family home, Pomurlo Vecchio, is an eccentric 12thC tower, jutting out of a wooded hillock. It also has four small apartments, each with its separate entrance. They are homely, though rather frayed at the edges and in need of redecoration.

The principal guest accommodation, however, Le Casette, stands on the other side of the estate, towards Baschi. Its three stone cottages have been recently rebuilt around a central swimming-pool on a hillside ridge. Though lacking the patina of age, they provide a summer oasis which is particularly suitable for families, Each room is simply decorated, with white plaster and exposed stone walls and comfortably furnished.

The restaurant, overseen by daughter Daniela, is noteworthy. Each course has a genuine farmhouse taste — 80 per cent of the ingredients are organically grown on the estate. This is complemented by the charm and warmth of the family, who eat with their guests and do everything to make them feel at home.

~

NEARBY Orvieto (15 km); Todi (20 km).
LOCATION 1 km S of SS448 near Lago di Corbara; or 5 km E of Baschi towards Montecchio
FOOD lunch, dinner
PRICE rooms (€); DB&B (€)-(€)(€) minimum stay one week in August
ROOMS 3 small apartments in main villa; 8 double rooms, 6 apartments in Le Casette complex (about 1 mile away); all with shower, refrigerator and breakfast
FACILITIES central heating; restaurant, bar; swimming-pool, horse-riding
CREDIT CARDS none **CHILDREN** welcome
DISABLED 3 bedrooms
PETS by prior arrangement **CLOSED** never
LANGUAGES some English
PROPRIETOR Lazzaro and Daniela Minghelli

TERNI

BASCHI

VILLA BELLAGO
~ COUNTRY HOTEL ~

Baschi, Strada per Todi (SS 448) 05023 Terni
TEL (0744) 950521 **FAX** (0744) 950524

UNDENIABLY MODERN, but stylish in its own way, Villa Bellago will appeal to travellers who enjoy contemporary comforts and the full range of facilities. Magnificently situated on the shores of Lago di Corbara, a man-made lake, the 'villa' was originally a set of 19thC farm buildings, but is now rigorously updated. The low-slung buildings, pleasantly rose-tinted, fit well into the tree-filled, undulating grounds that lead down to the lake. The interiors are defined by clean lines, occasionally broken by a traditional brick arch or fire-place. Furnishings are stylishly contemporary, and a minimalist approach to decoration gives a spacious feel.

The hotel certainly makes full use of its lakeside location: large picture windows carry your eyes over its rippling surface to the sloping green hills beyond. The gardens are meticulously cared for, with acres of rolling lawns and brightly coloured flowers in squat terracotta urns, and there is an outdoor pergola next to the restaurant where you can enjoy not just your meal and the view but also a cool evening breeze from the lake.

~

NEARBY Orvieto (10 km); Todi (15 km).
LOCATION lakeside locationon SS 448 between Orvieto and Todi; own grounds, ample car parking
FOOD breakfast, lunch, dinner
PRICE ⓔ-ⓔⓔ
ROOMS 10 double, 2 suites, all with bath or shower, phone, TV, minibar
FACILITIES sitting-room, bar,restaurant, garden, tennis court, swimming-pool, billiards, five-a-side football, gym, sauna
SMOKING permitted
CREDIT CARDS AE, DC, EC, MC, V **CHILDREN** welcome
DISABLED 2 adapted rooms **PETS** check when booking
CLOSED never; restaurant only, Tue
LANGUAGES English, French
MANAGER Massimiliano Benedetti

TERNI

NARNI

DEI PRIORI
~ TOWN HOTEL ~

Vicolo del Comune 4, Narni, 05035 Terni
TEL & FAX (0744) 726843

TUCKED AWAY IN A QUIET ALLEY in the medieval heart of one of southern Umbria's unsung towns, this friendly small hotel provides an ideal staging post for travellers who prefer the 'backroads' route along the vía Flaminia to Rome. As well as the magnificent Piazza dei Priori, the town's Romanesque duomo and the 14thC Palazzo del Podestà provide ample reason for an overnight detour.

The meat hooks in the bricked, vaulted ceiling of the entrance hall indicate that it was once the food store for the palazzo. Upstairs, the sitting-rooms on the piano nobile, with their carved stone architraves, are altogether more worthy.

A lift, or a grandiose black oval staircase, takes you up to the comfortable modern bedrooms which look out into the central courtyard or over the pantiled roofs of the medieval borgo. A few have their own small balconies.

Downstairs, the restaurant spills out into the courtyard in the summer months. Its menu is mainly Umbrian (the local pasta dish is manfricoli), although the Venetian chef adds the occasional northern dish.

~

NEARBY Ponte di Augusto (2 km); Otricoli (14 km).
LOCATION 20 m from the town's main Piazza dei Priori
FOOD Breakfast, lunch, dinner
PRICE rooms €
ROOMS 11 double, 5 single, 1 suite, all with shower, television, radio, minibar, central heating; 7 rooms with air-conditioning
FACILITIES sitting-room, breakfast room, bar, restaurant with tables also in the interior courtyard
CREDIT CARDS AE, DC, MC, V
CHILDREN accepted **DISABLED** no facilities
PETS small well-behaved animals accepted
CLOSED never **LANGUAGES** some English
PROPRIETOR Maurizio Bravi

Terni

Orvieto

La Badia
～ Old abbey ～

Loc. La Badia, Orvieto, 05019 Terni
Tel (07633) 01959 **Fax** (07633) 05396

ARRIVING AT TWILIGHT at La Badia is like landing in a scene from a Gothic novel: ruined arches, rooks cawing from a crenellated bell-tower, dark cypresses silhouetted against the sky and, across the valley, the evening profile of Orvieto's cathedral, secure on its fortress crag. But the golden stone monastery on the hill, surrounded by Umbria's intense green countryside, soon reveals itself as an outstanding hotel that would have delighted any Renaissance cardinal.

Restraint is the hallmark of this fine building's conversion into a distinctive hotel. The robust architecture of the old abbey is always allowed to speak for itself, and modern embellishments have been kept to a minimum. The heavy wooden period furniture goes well with the massive stone walls; wrought-iron lights illuminate vaulted ceilings; floors are either of plain or geometrically patterned terracotta. Here and there, an unexpectedly-placed church pew reminds the guest of what once was.

On the hill behind, is a pool fit for a pope. In front of the abbey, beside the famous 12-sided tower, is a peaceful garden where the meditative visitor can contemplate the view of Orvieto.

～

Nearby Orvieto (5 km); Todi (40 km); Viterbo (45 km).
Location on quiet hillside, 5 km S of Orvieto
Food breakfast, lunch, dinner
Price €€€-€€€€
Rooms 3 single, 16 double, 7 suites; all with bath or shower; all rooms have phone, air-conditioning, central heating
Facilities sitting-room, breakfast-room, bar, restaurant, conference-room, tennis-court, swimming-pool
Credit cards AE, V
Children welcome **Disabled** access difficult **Pets** not allowed
Closed Jan and Feb **Languages** English
Proprietor Luisa Fiume

TERNI

FATTORIA LA CACCIATA
~ COUNTRY VILLA ~

Loc. La Cacciata 6, Orvieto, 05010 Terni
TEL (0763) 300892-305481 **FAX** (0763) 341373

IT IS A SHORT DRIVE up from the small village of Canale, through rows of vineyards, to Villa La Cacciata. Across the valley stands Orvieto's cathedral, seated majestically on its limestone pedestal; the villa's swimming-pool must surely have one of the top ten locations in all of Italy.

The main building, an aristocratic villa with a 19thC facelift, remains the home of *avvocato* Belcapo and his family, while four stone farm buildings around it have been converted into simple guest accommodation. Each bedroom retains the atmosphere of a farm cottage: beamed and tiled ceilings and terracotta floors with simple, somewhat spartan, furnishings. Most of them have idyllic pastoral views out over the estate. Bathrooms are shared, but this is more than reflected in the low charges.

The Belcapo family's estate produces one of the area's premier Orvieto Classico wines and fine olive oil.

The kitchen and restaurant in one of the buildings are periodically used for cookery courses. For the remainder of the time, the family offer a tempting menu of strictly Umbrian fare.

~

NEARBY Orvieto's cathedral and Pozzo di San Patrizio (4 km)
LOCATION Near the village of Canale, S of Orvieto
FOOD breakfast, dinner on request
PRICE rooms (€); DB&B (€)
ROOMS 11 double rooms, sharing 10 bathrooms, central heating
FACILITIES sitting-room with television in each building, restaurant, bar; swimming-pool, garden, riding
CREDIT CARDS none
CHILDREN accepted
DISABLED no facilities
PETS not accepted
CLOSED Christmas period
LANGUAGES some English
PROPRIETOR Settimio Belcapo

TERNI

VILLA CICONIA
~ COUNTRY VILLA ~

Loc. Ciconia, Via dei Tigli 69, Orvieto, 05018 Terni
TEL (0763) 305582/3 **FAX** (0763) 302077

PROTECTED FROM THE NEARBY busy road and the encroachments of Orvieto's new suburbs by its tree-filled gardens, La Ciconia is a small, attractive 16thC grey stone villa with two bays of windows flanking an arched entrance. Inside, one encounters a variety of styles, from the spacious ground-floor public rooms with geometric, polychrome tiled floors, massive stone fireplaces and frescoed friezes to the simpler but more restful sitting-rooms on the upper floor, where leather couches add a zestful note of modernity.

The bedrooms are in a more rustic style, with wrought-iron or four-poster beds and antique chests that combine well with the exposed roof-beams and warm, terracotta floors. Bathrooms are spanking new and most have a shower rather than a bath.

The gardens are a delight, bounded by two streams. There is, unfortunately, some noise from the road outside. The restaurant serves Umbrian specialities with oil and wine from the owner's farms - popular for weddings, so it may get busy at weekends.

A pleasant alternative to La Badia (page 150) if the latter is full or you find it too expensive.

~

NEARBY Orvieto (3 km); Todi (33 km); Perugia (78 km).
LOCATION just outside Orvieto in its own grounds, ample car parking
FOOD breakfast, lunch, dinner
PRICE €€€-€€€€
ROOMS 9 double, 1 single, all with bath (one with Jacuzzi), phone, satellite TV, minibar, air-conditioning (L20,000 per day)
FACILITIES sitting-rooms, dining-room, breakfast-room, garden
CREDIT CARDS AE, DC, EC, MC, V
CHILDREN welcome **DISABLED** not suitable **PETS** please check first
CLOSED mid-Jan to mid-Feb; restaurant only, Mon
LANGUAGES English
PROPRIETOR Valentino Petrangeli

TERNI

TITIGNANO

FATTORIA DI TITIGNANO

RURAL HAMLET GUEST-HOUSE

Loc. Titignano, Orvieto, 05010 Terni
TEL (0763) 308022 **FAX** (0763) 308002

FATTTORIA DI TITIGNANO is not a place for people in search of refined luxury. It is a simple, honest, rural guest-house whose attractions are not those of a professionally run, starred hotel but of a working farm estate that gives a warm welcome.

Owned by the aristocratic Corsini family and set in two thousand hectares, the hamlet stands on a hillside overlooking the Tiber Valley and Lake Corbara. On one side of the wide street (when we visited, it was being paved with cobble-stones at the expense of the European Community) is the principal house containing the public rooms and some of the bedrooms. A lovely loggia on the first floor, overlooks the church and the former farm workers' cottages, where there are more bedrooms and a few small apartments.

The general style is battered rustic with hints of former elegance: carved stone doors and fireplaces, gloomy oil paintings and high wooden ceilings. Bedrooms vary in size and decoration: in the farmers' cottages, they are smaller and more modern, and the excellent bathrooms have been newly installed. Make a point of visiting the wine cellars and the cheese dairy.

NEARBY Orvieto (25 km); Todi (23 km)
LOCATION 25 km NE of Orvieto, off the SS 79 bis
FOOD breakfast, dinner
PRICE €
ROOMS 6 double, all with bath or shower; 5 apartments
FACILITIES sitting-room, dining-room, terrace, swimming-pool
CREDIT CARDS not accepted
CHILDREN welcome; 30% discount for 3rd bed in room
DISABLED not suitable **PETS** accepted
CLOSED never **LANGUAGES** English, French
MANAGERS Giulio and Monica Fontani

AREZZO

BIBBIENA

BORGO ANTICO
~ TOWN HOTEL ~

Via Bernardo Dovizi 18, Bibbiena, 52011 Arezzo
TEL (0575) 536445/46 **FAX** (0575) 536447

A USEFUL ADDRESS in a part of Tuscany not over-supplied with recommendable hotels in spite of the great countryside. Bedrooms are comfortable and modern. Public areas retain more of the character of the original palazzo. Golf, swimming, tennis, riding and a national park nearby.

FOOD breakfast, lunch, dinner **PRICE** € **ROOMS** 10 double, 2 single; all with shower, phone, TV, minibar **CREDIT CARDS** AE, V **CHILDREN** welcome **CLOSED** never **LANGUAGES** English French, German

CENTOIA

VILLA ELISIO
~ COUNTRY VILLA ~

Capezzine, 52040 Centoia Arezzo
TEL (0575) 613145 **FAX** (0575) 613167

A PEACEFUL OLD VILLA in the countryside a few miles west of Lake Trasimeno which puts to good effect the familiar formula of white walls, tiled floors, dark beams and mellow wooden furniture – as does the associated restaurant, Le Capezzine. Tennis and a swimming-pool. New to the guide: we would welcome reports.

FOOD breakfast lunch, dinner**PRICE** €€-€€€ breakfast € DB&B €€ **ROOMS** 11; all with bath or shower, TV, minibar **CREDIT CARDS** AE, DC, MC, V **CHILDREN** welcome **CLOSED** never **LANGUAGES** English

CORTONA

CORYS
~ COUNTRY HOTEL ~

Loc. Torreone, 7 Cortona, Arezzo
TEL (0575) 605141 **FAX** (0575) 631443

A USEFUL NEW STOPOVER address clinging to the hill just outside Cortona, whose charm is mainly in a stupendous view down the Valdichiana to Lake Trasimeno. Pleasant dining room with attractive lighting with outside dining also possible on the terrace to take in the view (expect nonresidents). Friendly small-hotel atmosphere, but nothing-special, standardised bedrooms. Recently restored, everything is new and spotless.

FOOD breakfast, lunch, dinner **PRICE** € **ROOMS** 7 double, all with bath or shower, phone, TV **CREDIT CARDS** AE. DC, MC, V **CHILDREN** welcome **CLOSED** never **LANGUAGES** English, French, German

AREZZO/FIRENZE

CORTONA

ITALIA
~ TOWN HOTEL ~

Via Ghibellina 5-7, Cortona, 52044 Arezzo
TEL (0575) 630254 **FAX** (0575) 630564

A CHEAPER ALTERNATIVE in Cortona to the San Michele. It does not have the same style, but it is very centrally located just a few steps from the main piazza. Furniture is a mixture of old and new and some of the bedrooms have stylish rustic antiques. Attractive rooftop terrace with views over the Valdichiana, and new restaurant, Taverna Il Ghibellina.

FOOD breakfast **PRICE** € **ROOMS** 26 rooms, 26 with bath or shower; all with phone, TV **CREDIT CARDS** EC, MC, V **CHILDREN** welcome (family rooms available) **CLOSED** mid-Nov to 7 Jan **LANGUAGES** little English spoken

CORTONA

LOCANDA DEL MOLINO
~ RESTAURANT WITH ROOMS ~

Loc. Montanare, Cortona, 52044 Arezzo
TEL (0575) 614192 **FAX** (0575) 614054

C ONVERTED MILL built of old stone situated between a stream and a road. Fortunately, most of the bedrooms look on to the quieter side and have comfortable furniture. Down-stairs is a pleasant sitting-room for guests and a restaurant, serving Tuscan and Umbrian specialities, decorated with old terracotta pots and dried flowers. Swimming-pool.

FOOD breakfast, lunch, diner **PRICE** €€ **ROOMS** 8 double, all with bath or shower, phone, TV, minibar **CREDIT CARDS** MC, V **CHILDREN** welcome **CLOSED** 10 Jan to 12 Feb **LANGUAGES** English

BAGNO A RIPOLI (FIRENZE)

IL PALAZZO
~ VILLA APARTMENTS ~

Via Vicinale di Paterno 3, Bagno a Ripoli, 50012 Firenze
TEL (055) 630127 **FAX** (055) 630127

O N THE HILLS of Bagno a Ripoli, 9 km SE of Florence stands this elegant 15thC villa with shady ornamental garden, and beyond that, a discreetly sited swimming-pool with a surprising view of Brunelleschi's cupola. Apartments are stylish and fully equipped. Nearby bus will take you to the centre.

FOOD self-catering **PRICE** € one-week minimum stay
ROOMS 5 apartments for 4-8 persons; **CREDIT CARDS** not accepted
CHILDREN welcome **CLOSED** never **LANGUAGES** English

FIRENZE

BARBERINO VAL D'ELSA (FIRENZE)

LA SPINOSA
~ FARM BED-AND-BREAKFAST ~

Via Le Masse 8, Barberino Val d'Elsa, 50021 Firenze
TEL (055) 8075413 **FAX** (055) 8066214

A GENUINE WORKING FARM now run on strict macrobiological principles without the use of herbicides or insecticides. The stone-built farmhouse has been decorated and furnished with considerable care and taste (apart from some garish fitted carpets). Swimming-pool and tennis available.

FOOD breakfast, lunch, dinner **PRICE** €€-€€€ **ROOMS** 4 double, 4 suites **CREDIT CARDS** V **CHILDREN** small **CHILDREN** welcome **CLOSED** Dec to Feb **LANGUAGES** English, French, German

CASTELFIORENTINO

CASTELLO OLIVETO
~ FARMHOUSE APARTMENTS ~

Via di Monte Olivo 6, Castelfiorentino, 50051 Firenze
TEL (0571) 64322 **FAX** (0571) 61508

T HE SETTING IS a magnificent castle of warm red brick that has played host to popes and royalty and is now mainly used for functions. Apartments are in nearby restored farmhouses surrounded by glorious countryside. Pool and tennis; summer concerts and medieval banquets in the castle.

FOOD none **PRICE** €€-€€€ **ROOMS** 8 apartments for 2-8 persons **CREDIT CARDS** EC, MC, V **CHILDREN** welcome **CLOSED** Nov **LANGUAGES** English

CERTALDO

OSTERIA DEL VICARIO
~ TOWN HOTEL ~

Via Rivellino 3, Certaldo Alto, 50052 Firenze
TEL (055) 668228 **FAX** (055)
E MAIL info@osteriadelvicario.it **WEB SITE** www.osteriadelvicario.it

N EXT TO THE PODESTÀ in hilltop Certaldo Alto is the Osteria del Vicario, occupying a former monastery which dates from the 13thC. This well-established restaurant also has a series of well-kept rooms, some of them in the main building and others in two nearby townhouses. Summer meals are served in the delightful pebble garden, which was once the monastery's cloister.

FOOD breakfast, lunch, dinner **PRICE** €-€€€ **ROOMS** 1 single, 12 doubles, 1 suite all with shower, TV, hairdryer; 5 have phones **CREDIT CARDS** AE, DC, EC, MC, V **CHILDREN** welcome **CLOSED** Jan (restaurant shut Wed) **LANGUAGES** English, French

FIRENZE

CORTINE

FATTORIA CASA SOLA
∽ COUNTRY HOUSE WITH APARTMENTS ∽

Loc. Cortine, Barberino Val d'Elsa, 50021 Firenze
TEL (055) 8075028 **FAX** (055) 8059194

M ONTARSICCIO, one of the old farm-houses on the Casa Sola estate (which produces chianti, olive oil and vin santo) has been pleasantly converted to apartments in classic Tuscan rustic style, each with its own garden area and access to the pool beside the main villa. Peaceful rural setting. Swimming pool, riding, mountain bikes.

FOOD dinner on request **PRICE** €-€€¡ (heating not included); minimum stay of one week Jun to Sep **ROOMS** 6 apartments sleeping from 2 to 8 persons **CREDIT CARDS** MC, V **CHILDREN** welcome **CLOSED** never **LANGUAGES** English, French, Spanish

DONNINI

VILLA PITIANA
∽ COUNTRY VILLA ∽

Loc. Pieve a Pitiana, Donnini, 50060 Firenze
TEL (055) 860259 **FAX** (055) 860326
E-MAIL pitiana@val.it **WEBSITE** www.val.it/aziende/ pitiana

A N ENORMOUS VILLA in the hills east of Florence. It offers 13 double bed-rooms and, be warned, 38 apartments. Heavy Empire style dominates, except in the medieval convent wing. Gardens and swimming-pool large enough not to make it seem too crowded. Elegant restaurant.

FOOD breakfast, dinner, snacks **PRICE** €€-€€€ (DBB available only, no single room rate) **ROOMS** 35 double, all with bath or shower, phone, TV, mini-bar **CREDIT CARDS** AE, DC, EC, MC, V **CHILDREN** welcome **CLOSED** Nov to Mar **LANGUAGES** English, French, German, Spanish

FIESOLE

FATTORIA DI MAIANO
∽ COUNTRY APAERTMENTS ∽

Via da Maiano 11, Fiesole, Firenze
TEL (055) 599600 **FAX** (055) 599640

O NLY 5 KM FROM Florence's centre, but, aside from the view (familiar to those who have seen the film *A Room with a View*) you could be in deep countryside. Classily furnished rustic apartments in farmhouses around imposing villa. Small swimming-pool and shop selling estate's own produce.

FOOD self-catering **PRICE** € (heating not included); 3-night min. stay; one week Mar to Oct **ROOMS** 7 fully equipped apartments for 2-10 persons **CREDIT CARDS** EC, MC, V **CHILDREN** welcome **CLOSED** never **LANGUAGES** English, French, German

FIRENZE

VILLA AURORA
~ TOWN HOTEL ~

Piazza Mino 39, Fiesole, 50014 Firenze
TEL (055) 59100 **FAX** (055) 59587
E-MAIL h.aurora@fi.flashnet.it **WEBSITE** www.villaaurora.com

L OCATED ON Fiesole's famous piazza just across from the cathedral in a
rambling 19thC villa with views from the rear terrace. Bedrooms vary
in size, quality and price; some have their own terraces. No. 7 bus to city
leaves outside the entrance. Busy bar next door can be noisy at night.

FOOD breakfast, lunch, dinner **PRICE** ©©-©©© **ROOMS** 23 double, 2 single, all
with bath or shower, phone, TV, minibar, safe **CREDIT CARDS** AE, EC, MC, V
CHILDREN welcome **CLOSED** never **LANGUAGES** English

VILLA BONELLI
~ TOWN HOTEL ~

Via F Poeti1, Fiesole , 50014 Firenze
TEL (055) 59513 **FAX** (055) 598942

A NOTABLE BARGAIN for accommodation in the centre of Fiesole (about two
minutes' walk to the main piazza and the bus to Florence). The
entrance, in a narrow side street, is rather dark, but the light improves on
the upper floors. Quaint old-fashioned furniture clashes with modern
pieces. Good restaurant with view.

MEALS breakfast, dinner **PRICE** ©-©©© **ROOMS** 23 rooms, all with bath or
shower, phone, TV, minibar, **CREDIT CARDS** AE, EC, MC, V **CHILDREN** welcome
CLOSED restaurant only, Nov to mid-Mar **LANGUAGES** English, French

ALBA
~ TOWN HOTEL ~

Via della Scala 22/38r, 50123 Firenze
TEL (055) 282610**FAX** (055) 288358
E-MAIL hotel.alba@firenzalbergo.it **WEBSITE** www.geoide.com/hotelalba

N OT FOR YOUR HONEYMOON, but a simple, clean, functional place to stay,
run by the friendly Caridi family in the historic centre close to the
railway station. Rooms are now sound proofed against noise from the busy
street. The breakfast-room is quite stylish except for the curtains on the
ceiling.

FOOD breakfast **PRICE** ©© **ROOMS** 24, all with bath or shower, phone, TV, minibar,
safe, air-conditioning **CREDIT CARDS** EC, MC, V **CHILDREN** welcome **CLOSED** never
LANGUAGES English, French

FIRENZE

FLORENCE

ALESSANDRA
City guest-house

Borgo SS. Apostoli 17, 50123 Firenze
Tel (055) 283438 **Fax** (055) 210619
E-mail info@hotelalessandra.com **Website** www.hotelalessandra.com

EXCELLENT LOCATION in a 16thC palazzo on a quiet street in the heart of Florence's historic centre is the main attraction of this modest pensione. Some larger rooms, suitable for families, are available at very reasonable prices.

Food breakfast **Price** €€ **Rooms** 6 single (2 with bath or shower), 19 double (14 with bath); some air-conditioned **Credit cards** AE, MC, V **Children** welcome **Closed** two weeks at Christmas **Languages** English, French

FLORENCE

APRILE
Town hotel

Via della Scala 6, 50123 Firenze
Tel (055) 216237 **Fax** (055) 280947

ORIGINALLY PALAZZO DEL BORGO, constructed in Medici times, and situated on a street leading away from Piazza S. Maria Novella, this hotel could have made more stylish use of its architectural inheritance. Still, there are vaulted ceilings (some frescoed), a shady courtyard and views of the church from some of the bedrooms

Food breakfast, snacks **Price** €€-€€€
Rooms 40, all with bath or shower, central heating, phone, minibar **Credit cards** AE, EC, MC, V **Children** welcome
Closed never **Languages** English

FLORENCE

ARIELE
Town hotel

Via Magenta 11, 50123 Firenze
Tel (055) 211509 **Fax** (055) 268521

FOUR BRIDGES down from the Ponte Vecchio, so not that central. Oscar Wilde would have had something cruel to say about the wallpaper in the sitting-room, but elsewhere it is usually simple white plaster enlivened with pottery and inoffensive paintings. Pleasant gravelled garden with palms and urns, either for breakfast or for a drink in the evening.

Food breakfast **Price** €-€€ **Rooms** 40, all with bath or shower, central heating, air-conditioning, TV **Credit cards** AE, EC, MC, V **Children** welcome **Closed** never **Languages** English

FIRENZE

FLORENCE

BOTTICELLI
~ TOWN HOTEL ~

Via Taddea 8, 50123 Firenze
TEL (055) 290905 **FAX** (055) 294322
E MAIL botticelli@italyhotel.com **WEB SITE** www.venere.it/firenze/botticelli

OCCUPYING TWO 'palazzi' (one dating from the 1600s with a frescoed, vaulted ceiling in the entrance), the Botticelli is near bustling San Lorenzo market. The bedrooms (some rather poky) are comfortable and modern, but original architectural features have been preserved where possible.

FOOD breakfast **PRICE** €-€€€ **ROOMS** 3 singles, 31 doubles or twins, all with bath or shower, phone, TV, air conditioning, minibar **CREDIT CARDS** AE, DC, EC, MC, V **CHILDREN** welcome **CLOSED** never **LANGUAGES** English, French

FLORENCE

CASCI
~ TOWN HOTEL ~

Via Cavour 13, 50129 Firenze
TEL (055) 211686 **FAX** 2396461
E-MAIL CASCI@pn.itnet.it **WEBSITE** http://www.emmeti.it/casci.html

CLOSE TO THE DUOMO and Palazzo Medici-Riccardi in a 15thC palazzo that once belonged to Rossini. However, Via Cavour is one of the city's main bus arteries so, notwithstanding the sound-proofing, ask for a quiet room at the back. Family run, with a welcoming atmosphere. Breakfast-room and bar have frescoed ceilings.

FOOD breakfast **PRICE** €-€€€ **ROOMS** 25 double, all with bath or shower, phone, TV **CREDIT CARDS** AE, DC, EC, MC, V **CHILDREN** welcome **CLOSED** never **LANGUAGES** English, French, German, Spanish

FLORENCE

CITY
~ TOWN HOTEL ~

Via S.Antonino 18, 50123 Firenze
TEL (055) 211543 **FAX** (055) 295451
E-MAIL info@hotelcity.net **WEBSITE** www.hotelcity.net

IN A BUSY SHOPPING STREET frequented by Florentine housewives and close to the San Lorenzo tourist market (leather goods and T-shirts) with its many restaurants. The hotel has been recently renovated, and while the style may not be to everyone's taste, at least there is a new, clean feel to it, with plenty of plants and colourful fabrics.

FOOD breakfast **PRICE** €€-€€€€ **ROOMS** 18, all with bath or shower, phone, TV, minibar, air-conditioning **CREDIT CARDS** AE, DC, EC, MC, V **CHILDREN** welcome **CLOSED** never **LANGUAGES** English, French, German,

FIRENZE

PLACE

DESIREE
~ TOWN HOTEL ~

Via Fiume 20, 50123 Firenze
TEL (055) 2382382 FAX (055) 291439

CLOSE TO THE STATION, which is convenient but not without its disadvantages, the Desiree is a small pensione, carefully managed by its owners, who have decided on a clean, simple approach with occasional touches of style. From the pleasant breakfast-room is a view of Florence's chaotic rooftops.

FOOD breakfast PRICE €-€€ ROOMS 26 double, all with bath or shower, phone, TV; 10 with air-conditoning CREDIT CARDS EC, MC, V CHILDREN welcome CLOSED 2 weeks in Aug LANGUAGES English

FLORENCE

MONTEBELLO SPLENDID
~ TOWN HOTEL ~

Via Montebello 60, 50123 Firenze
TEL (055) 2398051 FAX (055) 211867
E-MAIL hms@tin.it WEBSITE www.milanoflorencehotel.it

ON SIZE ALONE, we ought not to include this hotel, but its undeniable, studied elegance will appeal to many of our readers who are prepared to pay a little more. The style is neo-classical rather than Florentine, with subtle lighting and some fine antiques. Some rooms look on to garden.

FOOD breakfast, lunch, dinner PRICE €€€-€€€€ ROOMS 39 double, 13 single, 3 suites, all with bath or shower, phone, TV, minibar, air-conditioning CREDIT CARDS AE, DC, EC, MC, V CHILDREN welcome CLOSED never LANGUAGES English, French, German, Spanish

FLORENCE

PALAZZO BENCI
~ TOWN HOTEL ~

Via Pz. Madonna Aldobrandini 3, 50123 Firenze
TEL (055) 217049, 213848 FAX (055) 288308
E-MAIl palazzobenci@iol.it WEBSITE www.paginegialle.it/hotelbenci

THE 16THC PALAZZO of the historic Benci family has been converted – somewhat over-zealously, we think – to a modern hotel. Among its advantages are its prices, which are reasonable for the city centre and location close to the church of San Lorenzo. Elegant sitting- and breakfast-rooms. Bedrooms are standard, with modern comforts.

FOOD breakfast PRICE €€-€€€€ ROOMS 24 double, 11 single, all with bath or shower, phone, TV, minibar, air-conditioning, CREDIT CARDS AE, DC, EC, MC, V CHILDREN welcome CLOSED never LANGUAGES English, French, German

FIRENZE

FLORENCE

PENDINI
～ TOWN GUEST-HOUSE ～

Via Strozzi 2, 50123 Firenze
TEL (055) 211170 **FAX** (055) 281807
E-MAIL pendini@dada.it **WEBSITE** florenceitaly.net

BULL'S EYE LOCATION: you will see Pensione Pendini's sign on the wing of the 'new' (19thC) post office in Piazza Repubblica, where it occupies two storeys. Rooms are spacious: avoid those on the piazza, full of late-night cafés.

FOOD breakfast **PRICE** €€-€€€ (for triples and family suites) **ROOMS** 44, all with bath or shower, phone, TV, some air-conditioned **CREDIT CARDS** AE, DC, EC, MC, V **CHILDREN** welcome **CLOSED** never **LANGUAGES** English, French, German

FLORENCE

THE REGENCY
～ TOWN HOTEL ～

Piazza Massimo d'Azeglio 3, 50121 Firenze
TEL (055) 245247/2342936 **FAX** (055) 2346935
E MAIL info@regencyhotel.com **WEB SITE** www.regencyhotel.com

SOME MIGHT FIND the plush, opulent style of decoration used in this hotel rather overwhelming, although it is undeniably luxurious. Located slightly outside the historic centre of the city, it has the advantage of a cool and shady garden. The restaurant is well known for its sophisticated menu.

FOOD breakfast, lunch, dinner **PRICE** €€€€ **ROOMS** 30 double, 5 suites, all with bath or shower, phone, TV, safe, air conditioning **CREDIT CARDS** AE, DC, EC, MC, V **CLOSED** never

FLORENCE

LA RESIDENZA
～ TOWN HOTEL ～

Via Tornabuoni 8, 50123 Firenze
TEL (055) 284197 **FAX** (055) 284197 **E-MAIL** info@laresidenzahotel.com

VIA TORNABUONI is one of the most fashionable shopping streets in Italy, if not in Europe, where the price of a pair of shoes would cover five nights stay at La Residenza. So do not expect anything particularly chic, but enjoy the friendly atmosphere, the flowery roof terrace and the simple, value-for-money accommodation.

MEALS breakfast, dinner **PRICE** €-€€ **ROOMS** 24, all with bath or shower, phone, air-conditioning, TV, minibar **CREDIT CARDS** AE, DC, EC, MC, V **CHILDREN** welcome **CLOSED** never **LANGUAGES** English

FIRENZE

FLORENCE

ROYAL
∾ TOWN HOTEL ∾

Via delle Ruote 52, 50124 Firenze
TEL (055) 483287, 490648 **FAX** (055) 490976
WEBSITE www.paginegialle.it/royal05

A HOTEL REASONABLY CLOSE to the centre, with a large garden ensuring peace, is always worth knowing about in this overcrowded city. White marble fireplaces and polished wooden floors add elegance to public rooms. Bedrooms are more functional – the singles are small. Value for money.

FOOD breakfast **PRICE** €€-€€€ **ROOMS** 10 single, 30 double, all with bath or shower, phone, TV, minibar, air-conditioning, safe **CREDIT CARDS** AE, DC, EC, MC, V **CHILDREN** welcome **CLOSED** never **LANGUAGES** English, French, German, Dutch

FLORENCE

SILLA
∾ TOWN GUEST-HOUSE ∾

Via dei Renai 5, 50125 Firenze
TEL (055) 2342888
FAX (055) 2341437 **E-MAIL** hotelsilla@tin.it **WEBSITE** www.hotelsilla.it

E XCELLENT LOCATION in the quiet residential area of San Niccolo south of the Arno, but ten minutes' walk of the main sights. This old-fashioned pensione occupies the first floor of a 16thC palazzo and from its terrace you can see Florence's famous skyline. The decoration will not be to everyone's taste.

FOOD breakfast **PRICE** €€-€€€ **ROOMS** 36, all with bath or shower, phone, TV, safe, air-conditioning, minibar **CREDIT CARDS** AE, DC, EC, MC, V **CHILDREN** welcome **CLOSED** 2 weeks in Dec **LANGUAGES** English, French, German

FLORENCE

SPLENDOR
∾ TOWN HOTEL ∾

Via San Gallo 30, 50129 Firenze
TEL (055) 483427 **FAX** (055) 461276 **WEBSITE** www.hotelsplendor.it

C LOSE TO PIAZZA SAN MARCO and surprisingly swish public rooms for the price, with frescoed ceilings and chandeliers. The breakfast-room, where a copious buffet is served, has elegant painted panels. Bedrooms are more modern. There is a sunny terrace with a view of San Marco.

FOOD breakfast **PRICE** €€-€€€ **ROOMS** 31, most with bath or shower; all with phone, TV, safe, hairdrier **CREDIT CARDS** AE, EC, MC, V **CHILDREN** welcome **CLOSED** never **LANGUAGES** English, French, German

FIRENZE

VILLA BELVEDERE
~ SUBURBAN HOTEL ~

Via Benedetto Castelli 3, 50124 Firenze
TEL (055) 222501, 222502 **FAX** (055) 223163 **E-MAIL** villabelvedere@iol.it

HARDLY AN ARCHITECTURAL GEM, but a pleasant place to retreat to after a day's trekking around the city. Situated on the hill of Poggio Imperiale, beyond the old city gate of Porta Romana, surrounded by trees in well-kept gardens (with pool and tennis) and with views of the town, it has interiors which are modern and comfortable without being exciting.

FOOD breakfast, snacks **PRICE** €€-€€€ **ROOMS** 2 single, 21 double, 3 suites, all with bath or shower, phone, TV, safe, air-conditioning **CREDIT CARDS** AE, DC, EC, MC, V **CHILDREN** welcome **CLOSED** Dec to Feb **LANGUAGES** English

VILLA LIBERTY
~ TOWN HOTEL ~

Viale Michelangiolo 40, 50125 Firenze
TEL (055) 6810581 **FAX** (055) 6812595
E-MAIL info@hotelvillaliberty.com **WEBSITE** www.hotelvillaliberty.com

TURN-OF-THE-CENTURY villa with remnants of the Art Deco style of the period – decorated mirrors, stained glass and ornate lamps. Located some distance from the centre. Ask for a room on the garden side: at weekends, Viale Michelangiolo is busy until the small hours.

FOOD breakfast **PRICE** €€€ **ROOMS** 17 rooms, all with bath or shower, phone, TV, minibar **CREDIT CARDS** AE, EC, MC, V **CHILDREN** welcome **CLOSED** never **LANGUAGES** English, French, German

LA FATTORESSA
~ FARM GUEST-HOUSE ~

Via Volterrana 58, Galluzzo, 50124 Firenze
TEL (055) 2048418 **FAX** (055) 2048418

CONVENIENT IF YOU WANT to be close enough to Florence for day visits, but prefer to spend evenings in country surroundings. Rooms, available in the old casa colonica (farmhouse) and converted outbuildings, are simply furnished, clean and comfortable. Bus nearby goes to the centre, avoiding Florence's nightmare car parking.

FOOD breakfast, dinner (on request) **PRICE** €€ **ROOMS** 6 double (extra bed possible), all with bath or shower, heating **CREDIT CARDS** not accepted **CHILDREN** accepted **CLOSED** never **LANGUAGES** English, German, French

FIRENZE

GREVE

LA CAMPORENA
~ FARM GUEST-HOUSE ~

Via Figlinese 27, Greve in Chianti, 50022 Firenze
TEL (055) 853184, 8544765 **FAX** (055) 8544784

A LSO KNOWN AS Agriturismo Anna, located 3 km outside Greve on the road to Figline. A tree-lined drive leads up to this hilltop farmhouse, a position both peaceful and panoramic with views across the surrounding olive groves. Simple, cheap accommodation, with access to a pleasant garden and terrace.

FOOD breakfast, dinner **PRICE** € **ROOMS** 1 single, 15 double, all with bath or shower **CREDIT CARDS** AE, DC, EC, MC, V **CHILDREN** welcome **Closed** never **LANGUAGES** English, German, French

GREVE

CASA NOVA
~ FARM GUEST-HOUSE ~

Via Uzzano 30, Greve in Chianti, 50022 Firenze
TEL/FAX (055) 853459
E-MAIL casanova@chiantipop.net **WEBSITE** www.emmeti.it/toscana

T HE TOWN OF GREVE, capital of Chianti and scene of its annual wine fair, is getting closer to this typical Tuscan farm-house, but you will not notice – most of the views are of hilly countryside. Pleasantly proportioned rooms, some with their own terraces. Garden to sit in, with the old terracotta urns once used to store olive oil. A bargain.

FOOD breakfast **PRICE** € **ROOMS** 6 double, 4 with bath or shower, heating **CREDIT CARDS** EC, MC, V **CHILDREN** welcome **CLOSED** Jan/Feb to Mar **LANGUAGES** some English

GREVE IN CHIANTI

CASTELLO VICCHIOMAGGIO
~ CONVERTED CASTLE ~

Greve in Chianti, 50022 Firenze
TEL (055) 854079 **FAX** (055) 853911
E MAIL vicchiomaggio@vicchiomaggio.it **WEB SITE** www.vicchiomaggio.it

T HIS ANCIENT HILL-TOP CASTLE on a famous wine estate overlooks a landscape of vines, olive and cypress trees. Inside, the dimensions are impressive and possibly rather impersonal, and this goes also for the self-catering apartments. Huge dining room with vaulted ceilings.

FOOD breakfast, lunch, dinner **PRICE** €-€€€ **ROOMS** 3 double-bedded miniapartments, plus a further 4 sleeping four people each, all with bath, kitchen and heating **CREDIT CARDS** MC,V **CHILDREN** welcome **CLOSED** never **LANGUAGES** English, German, French

FIRENZE

CHIANTI
~ TOWN HOTEL ~

Piazza G. Matteotti 86, Greve in Chianti, 50022 Firenze
TEL (055) 853763, 853764 **FAX** (055) 853763

A FRIENDLY ATMOSPHERE and an enticing swimming-pool are the main attractions of this simple hotel located in Greve's principal piazza. The large entrance acts as reception, bar, sitting area and breakfast-room. Decent Tuscan food served in the more traditionally styled trattoria or on the back terrace.

FOOD breakfast, lunch, dinner **PRICE** €-€€ (for the suite) **Rooms** 15 double, 1 suite, all with bath or shower, phone, air-conditioning; some with TV **CREDIT CARDS** MC, V **CHILDREN** welcome **CLOSED** Nov **LANGUAGES** English, French

IL BURCHIO
~ FARMHOUSE CLUB ~

Via Poggio al Burchio 4, Incisa Valdarno, 50064 Firenze
TEL (055) 8330124 **FAX** (055) 8330234

R EACHED BY A WINDING dirt track, Il Burchio (a Club Ippico - riding club) is an informal, family-run country house in rustic style: white-washed walls, terracotta floors, wrought-iron bedsteads, wooden furniture and plenty of pretty floral fabrics. Traditional Tuscan meals are eaten at one table.

FOOD breakfast, lunch on request, dinner **PRICE** €-€€€ **Rooms** 1 single, 8 double, 2 suites; all with shower, TV on request
CREDIT CARDS EC, MC, V **CHILDREN** welcome **CLOSED** end Oct-end Mar
LANGUAGES some English

IL MOLINO DEL PONTE
~ COUNTRY APARTMENTS ~

Loc. Baccaiano, Via Volterrana Nord 16, Montespertoli, 50025 Firenze
TEL (0571) 671501 **FAX** (0571) 671435

A SOMEWHAT HEAVY-HANDED modernization takes away from the character of this centuries-old mill, with restaurant, below Montespertoli. To compensate, everything is spanking new in a contemporary Tuscan rustic style. Plenty of sporting activities available in the area (including an unattractive sports complex next door).

FOOD breakfast **PRICE** €-€€€ **Rooms** 4 double, 2 single, all with bath or shower, TV, minibar; 15 studio apartments **CREDIT CARDS** EC, MC, V **CHILDREN** welcome **CLOSED** never **LANGUAGES** English, French, German, Spanish

FIRENZE

PELAGO

LA DOCCIA
~ COUNTRY GUEST-HOUSE ~

19/20 Ristonchi, 50060 Pelago, Firenze
TEL (055) 8361387 **FAX** (055) 8361388
E-MAIL info@ladocciawelcomes.com **WEBSITE** www.ladocciawelcomes.com

A MORNING AND EVENING drop off and pick-up service to Pontassieve railway station for guests wanting a car-free day in Florence is just one of the advantages of this peaceful farmhouse. Run by the Mayhew family, it is set in woodlands and meadows high in the hills above the Arno valley. Traditionally furnished bedrooms, and a pool.

FOOD breakfast, light lunches, dinner **PRICE** ©©-©©© **ROOMS** 5 double, 3 suites, 2 villas, all with bath or shower **CREDIT CARDS** MC, V **CHILDREN** welcome **CLOSED** never **LANGUAGES** English

QUINTO ALTO

PODERE NOVELLETO
~ COUNTRY GUEST-HOUSE ~

Via Carmignanello 4, Quinto Alto, Sesto Fiorentino, 50019 Firenze
TEL (055) 454056 **FAX** (055) 451979

S ITUATED JUST BEYOND Florence's sprawling northern suburb of Sesto Fiorentino, Podere Novelleto is a delightful place to retreat to after a tough day at the city's overcrowded museums. Great view of the city from the pergola on the terrace. Rooms are simply furnished, some in rustic style.

FOOD breakfast, dinner **PRICE** ©-©© (DB&B) **ROOMS** 5 double, all with bath or shower **CREDIT CARDS** EC, MC, V **CHILDREN** welcome **CLOSED** never **LANGUAGES** English, German, French

RIGNANA

FATTORIA RIGNANA
~ COUNTRY GUEST-HOUSE ~

Loc. Rignana, nr. Badia a Passignano, Greve in Chianti, 50022 Firenze
TEL (055) 852065 **FAX** (055) 8544874

A T THE END of a long unsurfaced road (that starts at the lovely Badia a Passignano) lies this clutter of stone farmhouses and an 18thC villa among unspoilt Chianti countryside. Accommodation is simple but not unstylish (some without own bathroom, however), with the bonus of an excellent trattoria (closed Tue) with a fine view over the vineyards.

FOOD breakfast **PRICE** © **ROOMS** 7 double, 4 with own bath or shower; 2 apartments for four people **CREDIT CARDS** AE, V **CHILDREN** welcome **CLOSED** Nov to Mar **LANGUAGES** English, German, French

FIRENZE

RUFINA

FATTORIA DI PETROGNANO
~ FARM GUEST-HOUSE ~

Via di Petrognano 40, Pomino, Rufina, 50060 Firenze
TEL (055) 8318812, 8318867 **FAX** (055) 242918
E-MAIL lagoria@dada.it

MAGNIFICENTLY LOCATED high in the Rufina hills in the famous Pomino wine-making area, this is very much a place for those who like simple, unstuffy surroundings, a family atmosphere and fine views. Meals are served in the converted stables at a long communal table beneath white arches. Local train to centre of Florence (20 minutes).

FOOD breakfast, lunch (on request), dinner **PRICE** € **ROOMS** 7 double, most with bath or shower; 5 apartments for 2 to 10 people **CREDIT CARDS** AE, MC, V **CHILDREN** welcome **CLOSED** Nov to Easter **LANGUAGES** English, French

SAN CASCIANO

LA GINESTRA
~ FARMHOUSE APARTMENTS ~

Via Pergolato 3, San Pancrazio, 50020 Firenze
TEL/FAX (055) 8249245 **E-MAIL** laginestra@ftbcc.it

TRUE 'AGRITURISMO': a working farm producing organic produce, for its restaurant. Two isolated farmhouses are available, one divided into apartments (simple rustic style); the other takes groups of up to 13 people. Peace is assured – it's a long way even to the nearest bar.

FOOD lunch, dinner **PRICE** €-€€ **ROOMS** 5 apartments for 2-6; one house for 13 (heating not included), all with sitting/dining room, kitchen, bath, shower, heating, garden, pool **CREDIT CARDS** EU, MC, V **CHILDREN** welcome **CLOSED** never Languages English, German, French, Spanish

SAN CASCIANO VAL DI PESA

ANTICA POSTA
~ RESTAURANT-WITH-ROOMS ~

Piazza Zannoni 1/3, 50026 Firenze
Tel (055) 822313, 822247 **FAX** (055) 822278 **E-MAIL** anticaposta@ftbcc.it

A USEFUL TOURING BASE situated on the western edge of the Chianti Classico area, and convenient for Florence, Siena, San Gimignano and Volterra. More famous as a restaurant than a hotel, the rooms are modern and comfortable but not particularly stylish. Location on busy road not an advantage.

FOOD breakfast, lunch, dinner **PRICE** €-€€¡ **ROOMS** 3 single, 7 double all with bath or shower, TV **CREDIT CARDS** AE, EC, MC, V **CHILDREN** welcome **CLOSED** never; restaurant only, Tue (winter) **LANGUAGES** English, German, Spanish

FIRENZE

SAN DONATO IN FRONZANO

FATTORIA DEGLI USIGNOLI
∾ FARMHOUSE APARTMENTS ∾

San Donato in Fronzano, Donnini, Reggello, 50060 Firenze
TEL (055) 8652018 **FAX** (055) 8652270

A SPECTACULAR SETTING 350 m above the Arno Valley makes this hard to ignore, despite its large size and functionality. Apartments in the main farmhouse and outbuildings – all furnished in modern rustic style – are pleasant, but impersonal. Several restaurants, two pools, riding, games room.

FOOD breakfast, dinner **PRICE** ¡; DB&B ¡ **ROOMS** 40 mini-apartments, with 1 or 2 double bedrooms, shower, kitchenette, sitting/dining room, heating, phone **CREDIT CARDS** AE, EC, MC, V **CHILDREN** welcome **CLOSED** Nov to Easter **LANGUAGES** English, German

STRADA IN CHIANTI

VILLA LA MONTAGNOLA
∾ COUNTRY VILLA ∾

Via della Montagnola 110/112, Strada in Chianti, Firenze
TEL (055) 858485, 8587003 **FAX** (055) 858485

A SOLID 19THC VILLA which fronts the busy SS222 Chiantigiano road, but benefits from lovely views from its rear. Bedrooms are large, airy and, like the rest of the hotel, well kept. Public rooms are filled with polished wood furniture and a mixed bag of paintings. We found the atmosphere somewhat soulless – no complaints, but no buzz.

FOOD Breakfast **PRICE** €€ **ROOMS** 11 doubles, 2 suites; all have bath and shower, TV, minibar, heating, phone **CREDIT CARDS** MC, V **CHILDREN** welcome **CLOSED** never **LANGUAGES** English, French

TAVARNELLE VAL DI PESA

PODERE SOVIGLIANO
∾ COUNTRY GUEST-HOUSE ∾

Via Magliano 9, Tavernelle Val di Pesa, 50028 Firenze
TEL (055) 8076217 **FAX** (055) 8050770 **E-MAIL** sovigliano@ftbcc.it

T HERE IS A REASSURING AIR about this solid, typically Tuscan farmhouse with its massive walls and old-fashioned dovecot, set in the hilly countryside behind Tavarnelle. Simply furnished bedrooms have independent access to the garden where visitors can relax.

FOOD breakfast, dinner on request **PRICE** €€ (DB&B); 4-day minimum stay Rooms 5 double, not all with own bathroom; 1- and 2-bedroom apartments **CREDIT CARDS** AE, MC, V **CHILDREN** welcome **CLOSED** never **LANGUAGES** English, French, Spanish

FIRENZE/GROSSETO

VICO D'ELSA

LA VOLPAIA
~ FARM GUEST-HOUSE ~

Strada di Pastine, Vico d'Elsa, 50050 Firenze
TEL (055) 8073063 **FAX** (055) 8073170

VAL D'ELSA IS BECOMING almost as popular with tourists as the main Chianti drag with easy access to Florence, Siena, Volterra and San Gimignano. This square 16thC villa and converted farmhouse with pool offers a warm welcome and pleasantly decorated bedrooms. Riding. Half-board only.

FOOD breakfast, dinner **PRICE** €€ (DB&B), aperitivi and wine included **ROOMS** 10 rooms all with bath or shower **CREDIT CARDS** not accepted; travellers' cheques **CHILDREN** welcome **CLOSED** never **LANGUAGES** English, French

ANSEDONIA/GROSSETO

LOCANDA DI ANSEDONIA
~ ROADSIDE INN ~

Loc. Ansedonia, Via Aurelia Sud (140.5km), Orbetello Scalo, 58016 Grosseto
TEL (0564) 881317 **FAX** (0564) 881727

THE ADDRESS IMMEDIATELY gives away the main defect of this otherwise pleasant inn: it is very near the busy Rome-Grosseto highway. Double-glazing has been used to reduce the nuisance, but try to get a room looking on to the garden. A bargain, considering that it is only 15 km from the chic and costly resorts of Monte Argentario.

FOOD breakfast, lunch, dinner **PRICE** €-€€ **ROOMS** 1 single, 11 double, all with bath or shower, air-conditioning **CREDIT CARDS** AE, DC, EC, MC, V **CHILDREN** welcome **CLOSED** Feb **LANGUAGES** some English

MONTEMERANO/GROSSETO

VILLA ACQUAVIVA
~ COUNTRY HOTEL ~

Loc. Acquaviva, Montemerano, 58050 Grosseto
TEL (0564) 602890 **FAX** (0564) 602895

DEEP IN THE HEART of the Maremma and close to the thermal springs and mud-baths of Saturnia, this pleasant family-run hotel has been furnished with care and taste, using rustic antiques and bright fabrics. A garden with shady pines and a terrace, where in fine weather you can eat a delicious home-made breakfast, complete the picture. Tennis.

FOOD breakfast **PRICE** €€ **ROOMS** 25 double, all with bath or shower; 1 room for the disabled, 7 for smokers, 2 for pet owners **CREDIT CARDS** AE, EC, MC, V **CHILDREN** welcome **CLOSED** never **LANGUAGES** English

GROSSETO

RIFUGIO PRATEGIANO
~ MOUNTAIN HOTEL ~

Via Prategiano 45, Montieri, 58026 Grosseto
TEL (0566) 997703 **FAX** (0566) 997891

A 'RIFUGIO' IS NORMALLY a mountain hostel with basic facilities for tired walkers. This hotel, though still simple, has more to offer: a swimming-pool, restaurant, riding excursions and tennis, as well as an attractive location high in the Maremma hills. Hearty local food served.

FOOD Breakfast, lunch, dinner **PRICE** €-€€ **ROOMS** 4 single, 20 double, all with shower, phone, TV **CREDIT CARDS** EC, MC, V **CHILDREN** welcome **CLOSED** Nov to Easter **LANGUAGES** English

CALA DEL PORTO
~ SEASIDE HOTEL ~

Via del Porto, Punta Ala, 58040 Grosseto
TEL (0564) 922455 **FAX** (0564) 920716

B E PREPARED TO PAY for the pleasure of being at the centre of Tuscany's chic summer resort. Good facilities (pool, private beach), but you have to pay extra for tennis. Many of the bedrooms have their own terraces with a view of Elba. Staff can be rushed and impersonal in high season.

FOOD breakfast, lunch, dinner **PRICE** €€€€ (DB&B) Rooms 41 double, all with bath or shower, phone, TV, minibar **CREDIT CARDS** AE, DC, EC, MC, V **CHILDREN** welcome **CLOSED** Oct-May **LANGUAGES** English

PICCOLO HOTEL ALLELUJA
~ SEASIDE HOTEL ~

Via del Porto, Punta Ala, 58040 Grosseto
TEL (0564) 922050 **FAX** (0564) 920734

P UNTA ALA IS THE SUMMER HOME of the Tuscan jet-set, so be prepared to pay over the odds to stay in this yachting-and-boutique town of recent construction, especially in high season. The hotel is 'tasteful-modern' with a private beach. Rooms have either own terrace or private garden.

FOOD Breakfast, lunch, dinner **PRICE** ¡¡¡¡ (DB&B) Rooms 43 double, all with bath or shower, phone, TV, safe, minibar, air-conditioning **CREDIT CARDS** AE, DC, EC, MC, V **CHILDREN** welcome **CLOSED** Nov-Mar **LANGUAGES** English

GROSSETO/LIVORNO/LUCCA

SATURNIA/GROSSETO

VILLA CLODIA
~ COUNTRY VILLA ~

Via Italia 43, Saturnia, 58050 Grosseto
TEL (0564) 601212 **FAX** (0564) 601212

A TURN-OF-THE-CENTURY VILLA on the outskirts of the medieval village of Saturnia, ingeniously constructed around a limestone escarpment that gives great character to the interiors. Some bedrooms have access to a terrace overlooking the valley, and all can enjoy the morning sun pouring in to the light, airy breakfast-room. Thermal springs nearby.

FOOD breakfast **PRICE** €; 3-day minimum stay; Apr to Oct minimum stay 1 week **ROOMS** 2 single, 8 double, all with bath or shower, phone, TV **CREDIT CARDS** V **CHILDREN** welcome **CLOSED** 10-20 Dec **LANGUAGES** English

CASTIGLIONCELLO/LIVORNO

MONHOTEL
~ SEASIDE HOTEL ~

Via Aurelia 1023, Castiglioncello, 57012 Livorno
TEL (0586) 752570 **FAX** (0586) 752677

L IBERTY-STYLE VILLA dramatically perched above a rocky cove just outside Castiglioncello. Decent, unexciting interiors: you will stay here to enjoy the sea air, the private bathing area reached by a lift and the excellent sea-food restaurant. Most rooms have a view of the bay.

FOOD breakfast, lunch, dinner **PRICE** €€ **ROOMS** 35 rooms, all with bath or shower, phone, TV **CREDIT CARDS** AE, DC, EC, MC, V **CHILDREN** welcome **CLOSED** never **LANGUAGES** English, German, French

LUCCA (LUCCA)LUCCA

VILLA LA PRINCIPESSA
~ COUNTRY VILLA ~

Loc. Massa Pisana, Via Nuova per Pisa 1616, 55050 Lucca
TEL (0583) 370037 **FAX** (0583) 379136

T HE HEAVY EMPIRE STYLE is understandable when you realize that the villa was once the residence of the Dukes of Bourbon-Parma. Tartan (!) carpets, fabric-covered walls, gilt mirrors and draped tables give the interior an overladen air. Pleasant shady gardens and a swimming-pool. Traditional food served in the dramatic black dining-room.

FOOD breakfast, lunch, dinner **PRICE** €€€€-€€€€ **ROOMS** 5 single, 30 double, 5 suites, all with bath or shower, phone, TV, mini-bar, air-conditioning **CREDIT CARDS** AE, DC, EC, MC, V **CHILDREN** welcome **CLOSED** Nov-Mar **LANGUAGES** English, German, French

PISA

MONTOPOLI (PISA)

QUATTRO GIGLI
~ TOWN HOTEL ~

Piazza Michele da Monti 2, Montopoli 56020
TEL (0571) 466878 **FAX** (0571) 466879

MODEST BUT PLEASANT inn located in the central piazza of Montopoli, where it occupies a 14thC palazzo. More renowned as a restaurant than as a hotel, the bedrooms are fairly standardized; some have views of green valleys. In fine weather, dinner is served on a vine-shaded garden terrace by friendly staff.

FOOD breakfast, lunch, dinner **PRICE** € **ROOMS** 20 double, all with bath or shower, phone, TV, minibar **CREDIT CARDS** AE, DC, EC, MC, V **CHILDREN** welcome **CLOSED** 2 weeks in Nov **LANGUAGES** English, French

RIGOLI (PISA)

VILLA DI CORLIANO
~ COUNTRY VILLA ~

Via Statale 50, Rigoli, San Giuliano Terme, 56010 Pisa
TEL (050) 818193 **FAX** (050) 818341

USEFUL LOCATION for both Pisa and Lucca, and great value if the battered, aristocratic look is what you like. Public rooms are full of frescoes, chandeliers, statuary. Bedrooms are large but vary in standard; not all have bathrooms. Friendly atmosphere. Famous Pisan chef, Sergio, has a restaurant in the grounds. One visitor was impressed; another found it marred by a lack of comforts.

FOOD breakfast, lunch, dinner **PRICE** €€-€€€ **ROOMS** 18 double, 12 with bath or shower **CREDIT CARDS** EC, MC, V **CHILDREN** welcome **CLOSED** never **LANGUAGES** English

VOLTERRA

VILLA RIODDI
~ COUNTRY HOTEL ~

Loc. Rioddi, Volterra, 56048 Pisa
TEL (0588) 88053 **FAX** (0588) 88074

LARGE OPEN SPACES spanned by stone arches and brick-vaulted ceilings characterize the ground floor of this 15thC villa just outside Volterra. Furnishing is modern and standardized, with some reproduction rustic. Bedrooms are light, airy and fully equipped. New swimming-pool and garden.

FOOD breakfast **PRICE** €-€€ **ROOMS** 9 double, all with bath or shower, phone, TV; 3 apartments for 4 people **CREDIT CARDS** AE, DC, EC, MC, V **CHILDREN** welcome **CLOSED** 10 Jan to Mar **LANGUAGES** English

SIENA

PESCIA

MARZALLA
~ AGRITURISMO APARTMENTS ~

Via Collecchio 1, Pescia, 51017 Pistoia
TEL (0572) 490751 **FAX** (0572) 478332

THIS FAMILY-RUN Agriturismo has a pleasant setting in the Pistoiese hills, and offers value for money. The five apartments are simply but attractively decorated in rustic style; three have fire places and all have small private gardens. A separate restaurant provides wholesome Tuscan meals.

FOOD breakfast, dinner **PRICE** €€€€ (for 2 or for 8 people) per week **Rooms** 5 apartments available by the week (3 nights minimum off season); all rooms have bath, shower, TV, phone **CREDIT CARDS** not accepted **CHILDREN** welcome **CLOSED** never **LANGUAGES** English, French

BAGNO VIGNONI

POSTA MARCUCCI
~ COUNTRY HOTEL ~

Bagno Vignoni 53027, San Quirico d'Orcia, Siena
TEL (0577) 87712 **FAX** (0577) 887119

STRONGLY RECOMMENDED by a reader, the Posta Marcucci is new to the guide. It is a simple hotel in a quiet resort village in the middle of the Orcia Valley, equipped with comfortable bedrooms, spacious sitting-rooms and a pool filled by cascades of water from a thermal spring. Tennis, sauna, gym and bowls. Wonderful views, and good value.

MEALS breakfast, lunch, dinner
Prices ¡-¡¡ (DB&B) Rooms 46, all with bath or shower
Credit cards AE, EC, MC, V Children welcome Closed never Languages English, Spanish, German

BUONCONVENTO

FATTORIA PIEVE A SALTI
~ FARM GUEST-HOUSE ~

Loc. Pieve a Salti, Buonconvento, 53022 Siena
TEL (0577) 807244 **FAX** (0577) 807244

AN APPEALING CHOICE for those who like the outdoor life. Pieve a Salti is set in 550 hectares of farmland and hunting reserve which supplies the restaurant with oil, meat, game and cheese. Six fishing ponds are available for anglers and a swimming-pool for idlers. Rooms are distributed among the estate's farmhouses.

FOOD breakfast, lunch, dinner **PRICE** € (DB&B) **ROOMS** 1 single, 11 double, all with bath or shower **CREDIT CARDS** EC, MC, V **CHILDREN** welcome **CLOSED** never **Languages** English, French, German

SIENA

CASOLE D'ELSA

PIETRALATA
~ COUNTRY GUEST-HOUSE ~

Loc. Pietralata, Via del Teschio 8, Casole d'Elsa, 53031 Siena
TEL (0577) 948657 **FAX** (0577) 948468

LOVELY RAMBLING FARMHOUSE in classic Tuscan style 5 km outside town of Casole d'Elsa, reached by an unsurfaced road. Covered terraces look on to gardens. Bedrooms simply furnished with rustic antiques. Owner presides over communal dinner in a lovely brick-ceilinged dining-room.

FOOD breakfast, dinner **PRICE** ¡ **Rooms** 10 double, all with bath or shower
Credit cards not accepted **CHILDREN** reluctantly accepted
CLOSED never **LANGUAGES** English, German, French

CASTEL SAN GIMIGNANO

LE VOLPAIE
~ HOTEL TYPE ~

Via Nuova 9, Castel San Gimignano, 53030 Siena
TEL (0577) 953140 **FAX** (0577) 953142 **E-MAIL** levolpaie@iol.it
WEBSITE www.sangimignano.com/levolpaie

SMALL MODERN HOTEL, with swimming-pool, and not without hints of character, in the suburbs of the nondescript town of Castel San Gimignano. Suitable for an overnight stop if touring in this popular area. The friendly welcome, comfortable rooms, many with their own balconies, garden and reasonable prices make this a place not to be overlooked.

FOOD breakfast **PRICE** €-€€ **ROOMS** 12 double, 3 single, all with bath or shower,
phone, TV **CREDIT CARDS** AE, DC, EC, MC, V **CHILDREN** welcome
CLOSED 10 Nov to 10 Mar **LANGUAGES** English, some French

CASTELNUOVO BERARDENGA

PODERE COLLE AI LECCI
~ FARMHOUSE APARTMENTS ~

Loc. San Gusme, Castelnuovo Berardenga, 53010 Siena
TEL (0577) 359084 **FAX** (0577) 358914

THE DANISH OWNER of this old stone farmhouse makes one of the finest Chianti Classicos, and the house itself is classically Chianti in its location amidst vines, olives and cypresses. Some apartments have their own terraces; others have small private gardens. Wine and oil from the estate on sale.

FOOD self-catering **PRICE** €-€€ (heating L25,000 per day); one week minimum
stay **ROOMS** 3 apartments for 2-4 persons; each with kitchen/living room, bedroom
and bathroom **CREDIT CARDS** DC, V **CHILDREN** welcome **CLOSED** never
LANGUAGES English, Danish, German, French

SIENA

COLLE VAL D'ELSA

VILLA BELVEDERE
~ COUNTRY VILLA ~

Loc. Belvedere, Colle Val d'Elsa, 53034 Siena
TEL (0577) 920966 **FAX** (0577) 924128

THIS TIME-WORN OLD VILLA set in its own grounds operates chiefly as a restaurant (especially for weddings and other large functions). Heavy rustic style predominates throughout. Large, well-tended gardens. Food is excellent, and the guest-book is full of appreciative comments. The nearby busy road is a nuisance.

FOOD breakfast, lunch, dinner **PRICE** €-€€ **ROOMS** 15 double, all with bath or shower, phone, TV **CREDIT CARDS** AE, DC, EC, MC, V **CHILDREN** welcome **CLOSED** never **LANGUAGES** English

FONTERUTOLI

CASTELLO DI FONTERUTOLI
~ VILLAGE APARTMENTS ~

Loc. Fonterutoli, Castellina in Chianti, 53011 Siena
(bookings - Stagioni del Chianti, Via di Campoli 142, Mercatale V d Pesa, FI)
TEL (0577) 73571 (bookings) **FAX** (0577) 735757 (bookings)

THIS QUAINT STONE-BUILT village contains some stylishly converted and furnished apartments for weekly rent. Secluded, despite nearby Florence-Siena road (the Chiantigiana). Good restaurant in village that also sells local produce. Swimming-pool.

FOOD self-catering apartment **PRICE** €; one-week minimum stay **ROOMS** 6 fully-equipped apartments for 4-8 persons **CREDIT CARDS** not accepted **CHILDREN** welcome **CLOSED** never **LANGUAGES** English

MODANELLA

FATTORIA GODIOLO
~ FARM-GUEST-HOUSE ~

Via Modanella Godiolo 22, Rapolano Terme, 53040 Siena
TEL/FAX (0577) 704304

YOU WILL BE CHARMED by the fine upper and lower loggias and tower that form the central part of this old farmhouse devoted to the making of wine, honey and olive oil. Each bedroom has been carefully and individually decorated. Breakfast is with home-made products, and dinner is worth requesting. Useful base for visiting Siena (30 km), Arezzo and Cortona.

FOOD breakfast, dinner on request **PRICE** €€ **ROOMS** 3 double, all with bath or shower **CREDIT CARDS** not accepted **CHILDREN** welcome **CLOSED** never

SIENA

MONTEPULCIANO

IL RICCIO
~ TOWN GUEST-HOUSE ~

Via Talosa 21, Montepulciano, 53045 Siena
TEL (0578) 757713 **FAX** (0578) 757713

LOCATED RIGHT IN THE CENTRE of the historic town of Montepulciano, near the Piazza Grande, in an old building going back to the 13thC. Recent restoration has unfortunately removed much of the original character.

FOOD breakfast **PRICE** € **ROOMS** 5 double, all with bath or shower, phone, TV **CREDIT CARDS** AE, MC, V **CHILDREN** welcome **CLOSED** first 10 days in June, first 10 days in Nov **LANGUAGES** some French

MONTERIGGIONI

CASTEL PIETRAIO
~ CASTLE APARTMENTS ~

Loc. Castel Pietraio, Monteriggioni, 53035 Siena
(Via de' Fusari 13, 40123 Bologna – for bookings)
TEL (0577) 301038; (051) 267534 **FAX** (051) 221376 (bookings)
E-MAIL m.delnero@tin.it **WEBSITE** www.castelpietraio.it

SOLID APARTMENTS for Tuscan enthusiasts in this imposing, even forbidding, grey medieval stone structure, a few kilometres away from the more elegant defenses of Monteriggioni. Not much to do locally but a good base for reaching Siena, Florence, San Gimignano and Volterra.

FOOD self-catering **PRICE** €€; minimum stay: 2 days Oct-May; 1 week Jun-Sep **ROOMS** 6 double, 2 suites; 7 full-equipped apartments for 3-5 persons; no pets allowed **CREDIT CARDS** AE, MC, V **CHILDREN** welcome **CLOSED** never **LANGUAGES** little English spoken

MONTICIANO

LOCANDA DEL PONTE
~ COUNTRY HOTEL ~

Loc. Ponte a Macereto, Monticiano, 53015 Siena
TEL (0577) 757108 **FAX** (0577) 757110

17THC INN THAT USED TO BE a stopping-point for the Italian post (nobody knows where it stops now). The best rooms look on to the River Merse and the ruined bridge that gave the locanda its name, now the site of the hotel's private river beach. Elegant rustic style and appetising food will persuade visitors to use it for longer than an overnight stay.

FOOD breakfast, lunch, dinner **PRICE** €€-€€€ **ROOMS** 23 double, all with bath or shower, phone, TV, minibar, air-conditioning **CREDIT CARDS** AE, DC, EC, MC, V **CHILDREN** welcome **CLOSED** Feb **LANGUAGES** English, German, French

SIENA

MONTI IN CHIANTI

LOCANDA DEL MULINO
～ FARM GUEST-HOUSE ～

Loc. Mulino delle Bagnaie, Monti in Chianti, 53010 Siena
TEL/FAX (0577) 747103

SIMPLE AND HOSPITABLE converted mill, off the main road between Gaiole and Siena (SS 408). Attractive bedrooms in rustic style have access to the grounds which lead down to a river. Breakfast is in the old mill itself, machinery still intact.

FOOD breakfast, dinner on request (30,000 lire incl. wine) **PRICE** ⓔ **ROOMS** 5 double, all with bath or shower; heating **CREDIT CARDS** not accepted **CHILDREN** welcome (50 per cent discount for under-12s) **CLOSED** Nov to Mar **LANGUAGES** English, French

QUERCEGROSSA

MULINO DI QUERCEGROSSA
～ COUNTRY GUEST-HOUSE ～

Via Chiantigiana, Quercegrossa, 53011 Siena
TEL & FAX (0577) 328129

A CONVERTED MILL, off the Chiantigiana (the old Florence-Siena road) surrounded by paved and terraced gardens. A large restaurant and ice-cream parlour make for a lively atmosphere. Prices are reasonable, and the furnishing is a good example of the modern 'rustic' style. Only 8 km from Siena and an hour's drive from Florence.

FOOD breakfast, dinner **PRICE** ⓔ **ROOMS** 12 double, all with bath or shower **CREDIT CARDS** MC, V **CHILDREN** welcome **CLOSED** Jan to mid-Mar **LANGUAGES** English, French

QUERCEGROSSA

VILLA GLORIA
～ COUNTRY VILLA ～

Loc. Quercegrossa, 53010 Siena
TEL (0577) 327103 **FAX** (0577) 327004

RAMBLING hillside villa just off the old road from Florence to Siena (Chiantigiana) and only 5 km from the latter. Smart interiors belie the 16thC origins of the farmhouse, which has been converted and furnished with a light hand. Panoramic terrace for breakfast and a swimming-pool for relaxation. Value for money.

FOOD breakfast **PRICE** ⓔ-ⓔⓔ **ROOMS** 26 double, all with bath or shower, phone, TV; 5 mini-apartments for 2-5 persons **CREDIT CARDS** AE, DC, EC, MC, V **CHILDREN** welcome **CLOSED** Nov **LANGUAGES** English

SIENA

CASTELLO DI VOLPAIA
~ COUNTRY APARTMENTS ~

Loc. Volpaia, Radda in Chianti, 53017 Siena
TEL (0577) 738066 **FAX** (0577) 738619

FORTIFIED HILLTOP VILLAGE in deepest Chianti, now sadly 'discovered' by tourists. It produces some prestigious wines, and offers a few compact apartments. Nearby is the Podere Casetto, more spacious, and with private garden and pool. A quaint bar/grocery in the village sells everyday essentials, local produce and snacks.

FOOD self-catering apartments **PRICE** €€ **ROOMS** 4 apartments and a farmhouse (with own pool), for 2-8 persons **CREDIT CARDS** AE, MC, V **CHILDREN** welcome **CLOSED** never **LANGUAGES** English, German

CANTINA IL BORGO
~ FORMER COACH-HOUSE ~

Rocca d'Orcia, 53027 Siena
TEL (0577) 887280 **FAX** (0577) 887280

CLOSE TO THE THERMAL SPRINGS of Bagno Vignoni and not far from Pienza, you will find, in the central piazza of this well-preserved medieval hamlet, the restaurant Cantina Il Borgo, which, as well as serving delicious local food, also has a few stylishly decorated bedrooms for visitors. Used to be the coach-house.

FOOD breakfast, lunch, dinner **PRICE** € **ROOMS** 3 double, all with bath or shower, air-conditioning **CREDIT CARDS** AE, EC, MC, V **CHILDREN** welcome **CLOSED** Feb and one week Nov **LANGUAGES** English, German

IL CASOLARE DI LIBBIANO
~ COUNTRY GUEST-HOUSE ~

Loc. Libbiano 3, San Gimignano, 53037 Siena
TEL & FAX (0577) 955102 **FAX** (0577) 955102

CAREFULLY RESTORED and tastefully furnished old farmhouse which combines the advantages of country seclusion with easy access to San Gimignano and Siena. But if you do not feel like moving, there is a swimming-pool and excellent local cuisine on the spot. Bikes for hire.

FOOD breakfast, dinner **PRICE** €€ **ROOMS** 6 double, all with bath or shower, central heating **CREDIT CARDS** AE, MC, V **CHILDREN** welcome **CLOSED** Nov to Mar **LANGUAGES** English

SIENA

LA FORNACE DI RACCIANO
~ CONVERTED FARMHOUSE ~

Loc. Racciano 6, San Gimignano, 53037 Siena
TEL (0577) 942156 **FAX** (0577) 942156

COMFORTABLE CONVERTED FARMHOUSE in the countryside just outside San Gimignano, with a view of the famous towers. The owners have wisely stuck to the well-tried formula of terracotta, beams, brick and plaster, with no fancy touches. Also has an alluring pool, which makes it an excellent bargain for this popular area.

FOOD breakfast **PRICE** €-€€ **ROOMS** 5 double; all with bath or shower, TV, minibar **CREDIT CARDS** EC, MC, V **CHILDREN** welcome **CLOSED** Nov to Feb (except Christmas) **LANGUAGES** English, French

IL MATTONE
~ FARM GUEST-HOUSE ~

Loc. Mattone, (strada per Ulignano), San Gimignano, 53037 Siena
TEL & FAX (0577) 950075

ON A HILL, 5 KILOMETRES north-east of San Gimignano, with panoramic views. Il Mattone is a wine- and olive-producing agriturismo. Two farm buildings have been turned into a pleasant arrangement of bedrooms and apartments with their own little gardens, and all sharing a kitchen, dining and sitting area. Swimming-pool and tennis court.

FOOD breakfast **PRICE** €-€€ **ROOMS** 6 double, 4 apartments, all with bath or shower **CREDIT CARDS** not accepted **CHILDREN** welcome **CLOSED** never **LANGUAGES** English

MONCHINO
~ COUNTRY GUEST-HOUSE ~

Loc. Casale 12, San Gimignano, 53037 Siena
TEL (0577) 941136 **FAX** (0577) 943042

A DIRT TRACK BRINGS YOU to this old farmhouse (parts of which date back to the 15thC), about 3 km east of San Gimignano. The neat garden, filled with flower pots, has views over the vines to the town. Simple, light rooms in the converted hay-barn; those in the house have more character. Attractively situated swimming-pool just below the garden. Archery.

FOOD breakfast **PRICE** € **ROOMS** 10 doubles, all with bath or shower, minibar **CREDIT CARDS** not accepted **CHILDREN** welcome (only one family room available) **CLOSED** Dec to Feb **LANGUAGES** English, French

SIENA

PODERE MONTESE
～ FARM GUEST-HOUSE ～

Loc. Fugnano, Via Cellole 11, San Gimignano, 53037 Siena
TEL (0577) 941127 **FAX** (0577) 907350/938856

DRAMATICALLY SITUATED on a hillside 1.5 km north of San Gimignano. Visitors will appreciate the warm welcome and complete peace and quiet of Podere Montese as well as its swimming-pool complete with panoramic view. Rooms are modest but pleasant, with white-tiled floors and modern rustic furniture. The garden terrace makes a pleasant spot.

FOOD breakfast **PRICE** € **ROOMS** 9 double, all with bath or shower
CREDIT CARDS not accepted **CHILDREN** welcome **CLOSED** Nov to Mar
LANGUAGES English, German, French

PODERE VILLUZZA
～ COUNTRY BED-AND-BREAKFAST ～

Loc. Strada 25, San Gimignano, 53037 Siena
TEL (0577) 940585 **FAX** (0577) 942247 **E-MAIL** viluzza@tin.it

A SIMPLE FARMHOUSE with a few rooms to offer guests, at the end of an unsurfaced road 3 km north of San Gimignano. Podere Villuzza is very much a working farm, with vines growing practically to the door. Nothing fancy about the accommodation, just pleasant, honest hospitality in a genuine rural setting and at reasonable prices. Swimming-pool.

FOOD breakfast, dinner on request **PRICE** €€ **ROOMS** 4 doubles, all with shower, heating; 3 mini-apartments with sitting-room and cooking corner
CREDIT CARDS AE, MC, V **CHILDREN** welcome **CLOSED** never **LANGUAGES** English, French

SAN MICHELE
～ COUNTRY HOTEL ～

Loc. Strada 14, San Gimignano, 53037 Siena
TEL (0577) 940596 **FAX** (0577) 940596

BRIGHT, UP-TO-DATE interiors and the clean lines of the public areas quickly establish the unfussy style of this hotel. Bedrooms are not very large but are well furnished, albeit not individually, and each has a new, modern bathroom. Rooms available for the disabled. Enjoyment of the garden diminished somewhat by the nearby road.

FOOD breakfast **PRICE** €-€€ **ROOMS** 14 double all with bath or shower, phone, TV **CREDIT CARDS** EC, MC, V **CHILDREN** welcome **CLOSED** 8 Jan to 15 Mar
LANGUAGES English, French, German

SIENA

SAN GIMIGNANO

SOVESTRO
~ COUNTRY HOTEL ~

Loc. Sovestro 63, San Gimignano, 53037 Siena
TEL (0577) 943153 **FAX** (0577) 943089

JUST OFF THE BUSY APPROACH road to San Gimignano (from Poggibonsi) about 2 km out of town. Contemporary hotel decoration predominates, though not without hints of style, such as the Montechi cotto floor tiling. All rooms have either a balcony or a private garden area. Swimming-pool.

FOOD breakfast, lunch, dinner **PRICE** €-€€ **ROOMS** 1 single, 40 double, all with bath or shower, phone, TV, air-conditioning **CREDIT CARDS** AE, DC, EC, MC, V **CHILDREN** welcome **CLOSED** Feb **LANGUAGES** English, French, German

SAN GIMIGNANO

VILLA BACIOLO
~ FORMER FARMHOUSE ~

Loc. San Donato, San Gimignano, 53037 Siena
TEL & FAX (0577) 942233

REASONABLY PRICED, simple guest-house only 4 km from San Gimignano, with a shady garden and the inevitable view which you can enjoy with your breakfast on the terrace. Restoration has been unobtrusive. Bedrooms are surprisingly stylish. Impressive brick-vaulted ceilings.

MEALS breakfast **PRICE** €; breakfast L9000 **ROOMS** 8 double, 1 single, all with bath or shower **CREDIT CARDS** not accepted **CHILDREN** welcome **CLOSED** Nov to Mar **LANGUAGES** English, German, French

SAN GIMIGNANO

VILLA BELVEDERE
~ COUNTRY HOTEL ~

Via Dante 14, San Gimignano, 53037 Siena
TEL (0577) 940539 **FAX** (0577) 940327

A 19THC VILLA redecorated in a light, contemporary style which will appeal to those who prefer modern comfort to time-worn individuality. Gardens are well laid out, with palms, olives, cypresses and rosemary bushes, but too close to a busy road for true seclusion. The swimming-pool is a bonus at these reasonable prices.

MEALS breakfast, dinner **PRICE** € **ROOMS** 1 single, 11 double all with bath or shower, phone, TV, minibar **CREDIT CARDS** AE, DC, EC, MC, V **CHILDREN** welcome **CLOSED** never **LANGUAGES** English, German

SIENA

SARTEANO

SANTA CHIARA
~ CONVERTED CONVENT ~

Piazza Santa Chiara, Sarteano, 53047 Siena
TEL (0578) 265412 **FAX** (0578) 266849
E-MAIL rsc@cyber.dada.it **WEBSITE** www.cybermarket.it/rsc

A 16THC CONVENT stylishly converted into a restaurant and hotel. The walled garden has an uninterrupted view of the Valdichiana. Furnishings and decoration show an eclectic mix of styles, with the rustic dominant. The restaurant, spanned by brick arches, concentrates on Tuscan cooking.

FOOD breakfast, dinner **PRICE** €€-€€€ **ROOMS** 9 double, 1 suite, all but two with bath or shower **CREDIT CARDS** DC, EC, MC, V **CHILDREN** welcome **CLOSED** 10 days in Feb and Nov **LANGUAGES** English

SIENA

SANTA CATERINA
~ TOWN HOTEL ~

Via Enea Silvio Piccolomini 7, 53100 Siena
TEL (0577) 221105 **FAX** (0577) 271087
E-MAIL hsc@sienanet.it **WEBSITE** www.sienanet.it-hsc

ALTHOUGH JUST ON THE WRONG SIDE of the city walls of Siena, this hotel is always popular. Best bedrooms are on the garden side, with views of the valley and the city while those facing the street have some sound-proofing. Antique furnishing in keeping with the building's character, and marble fireplaces add a welcome note of style.

FOOD breakfast **PRICE** €-€€ **ROOMS** 15 double, 4 single, all with bath or shower, phone, air-conditioning, TV, minibar **CREDIT CARDS** AE, DC, EC, MC, V **CHILDREN** welcome **CLOSED** never **LANGUAGES** English, French, German

SIENA

VILLA SCACCIAPENSIERI
~ TOWN VILLA ~

Via di Scacciapensieri 10, 53100 Siena
TEL (0577) 41441 **FAX** (0577) 270854
E-MAIL villasca@tin.it **WEBSITE** www.web.tin.it/villascacciapensieri

ON A HILLTOP 2 km north-east of Siena's historic centre, this 19thC villa has views of both the city's enchanting skyline and the peaceful Tuscan countryside. A formal garden with box hedges keeps at bay recent suburban development. Bedrooms large but unexciting. Shady terrace and pool.

FOOD breakfast, lunch, dinner **PRICE** €€-€€€€ **ROOMS** 23 double, 4 single, 4 suites, all with bath or shower, phone, TV, minibar, air-conditioning **CREDIT CARDS** AE, DC, EC, MC, V **CHILDREN** welcome **CLOSED** early Jan to mid-Mar, mid-Nov to 26 Dec **LANGUAGES** English, German, French

PERUGIA

HOTEL ALEXANDER
~ TOWN HOTEL ~

Piazza Chiesa Nuova 6, Assisi, 06081 Perugia
TEL (075) 816190 **FAX** (075) 816804

THIS SMALL FAMILY-RUN hotel is tucked away just off the central Piazza del Comune, and offers a useful alternative to Assisi's pricier central hotels. Its moderate-sized bedrooms have beamed ceilings and reproduction rustic furniture. Breakfast is served in the rooms. The Alexander is being renovated and extended as we go to press, which we understand will add much to the attractions. Reports welcomed.

FOOD no bar or restaurant facilities **PRICE** rooms € excl breakfast **ROOMS** 10 double, 1 suite **CREDIT CARDS** not accepted **CHILDREN** accepted **CLOSED** never **LANGUAGES** English

COUNTRY HOUSE
~ COUNTRY GUEST-HOUSE ~

San Pietro Campagna 178, Assisi, 06081 Perugia
TEL & FAX (075) 816363

THIS DELIGHTFUL stone-built guest-house, just below the walls of Assisi, combines proximity with rural tranquillity. Signora Silvana Ciammarughi furnishes the comfortable bedrooms from the stock of the antiques business which she runs downstairs. Several guests have found her friendly; some have been put off by her temperamental manner.

FOOD breakfast **PRICE** €-€€ with breakfast **ROOMS** 15, all with bath, central heating. **CREDIT CARDS** AE, V, MC **CLOSED** never **LANGUAGES** English, French, German

VILLA GABBIANO
~ COUNTRY VILLA ~

Loc. Gabbiano, Assisi, 06081 Perugia
TEL & FAX (075) 8065278

THE COUNTRY VILLA of Assisi's ancient Fiumi-Sermattei family stands in their 150-acre olive estate and has been run as a guest-house for more than a decade. The present major rebuilding work, planned for completion in spring 1996, should make it one of the area's most delightful country guest-houses. Reports welcome.

FOOD breakfast, dinner **PRICE** DB&B €-€€ **ROOMS** 9 doubles, 5 singles, 2 apartments in annex **FACILITIES** sitting-room, restaurant **CREDIT CARDS** none **CLOSED** never **LANGUAGES** French, some English

PERUGIA

CASTIGLIONE DEL LAGO

MIRALAGO
~ TOWN HOTEL ~

Piazza Mazzini 6, Castiglione del Lago, 06061 Perugia
TEL (075) 951157 **FAX** (075) 951924

DESPITE CENTRAL POSITION on main piazza, the quiet, spacious rear bedrooms have uninterrupted views over Lake Trasimeno. Most months,
the downstairs restaurant, serving fish from the lake as well as meatier,
Umbrian dishes, spills on to the lake-view terrace. Proprietors: Patrizi
family.

FOOD restaurant and bar **PRICE** rooms ⓔ **ROOMS** 19 doubles with shower, TV, air-
conditioning, minibar, central heating **Credit cards** DC ,V, MC
CHILDREN accepted **CLOSED** never

CITTÀ DI CASTELLO

LE MURA
~ TOWN HOTEL ~

Via Borgo Farinario 24, Città di Castello, 06012 Perugia
TEL (075) 8521070 **FAX** (075) 8521350

OCHRE STUCCOED WALLS and shuttered windows, which blend with the surrounding cottages, conceal the hotel's modern construction. Inside,
there is no such pretence – comfort and efficiency are regarded as more
important. The rear bedrooms have balconies which peep out over the
parapet of the city's medieval wall.

FOOD breakfast, lunch, dinner **PRICE** rooms ⓔ (breakfast included) **ROOMS** 30
double, 5 single, all with bath or shower, TV, minibar, air-conditioning and central
heating **CREDIT CARDS** AE, DC, MC, V **CHILDREN** accepted
CLOSED never **LANGUAGES** English, French

COLLAZZONE

ABBAZIA DEL COLLEMEDIO
~ CONVERTED MONASTERY ~

Loc. Collepepe, Via Convento, Collazzone, 06050 Perugia
TEL (075) 8789352 **FAX** (075) 8789324

A CONVERTED MONASTERY in the middle of the countryside between Todi
and Perugia which has all the facilities you could wish for, though
some might not like the holiday-camp atmosphere. Many attractive original features remain (such as bedrooms made out of monks' cells) but it
definitely has the air of a busy hotel. Kidney-shaped swimming-pool.

FOOD breakfast, lunch, dinner **PRICE** ⓔ ⓔ-ⓔ ⓔ ⓔ **ROOMS** 57 double, all with bath
or shower **CREDIT CARDS** AE, DC, EC, MC, V **CHILDREN** welcome

PERUGIA

GUALDO CATTANEO

IL ROTOLONE
~ COUNTRY GUEST-HOUSE ~

Loc. Sant'Anna, Gualdo Cattaneo, 06035 Perugia
TEL (0742) 91992 **FAX** (0742) 361307

THIS SMALL GUEST-HOUSE, housed in old farm-workers' cottages on the Benincasa family estate, commands fine views out over wooded hills towards Assisi. The moderate-sized bedrooms are simply furnished in appropriate country style. The dinner menu makes imaginative use of the farm's organically grown vegetables.

LOCATION between Gualdo Cattaneo and Bevagna **FOOD** breakfast, lunch, dinner **PRICE** rooms € with breakfast; DB&B ¡ **ROOMS** 8, all with shower, TV, heating Facilities sitting-room, restaurant, bar; garden, riding **CREDIT CARDS** accepted **CLOSED** never **LANGUAGES** some English, French

GUBBIO

BOSONE PALACE
~ TOWN HOTEL ~

Via XX Settembre 22, Gubbio, 06024 Perugia
TEL (075) 9220688 **FAX** (075) 9220552

THE CENTRE OF GUBBIO is not exactly brimming over with great hotels but the Bosone Palace is a convenient, reasonably priced place to stay. Attractive entrance and decorated breakfast-room with vaulted ceiling. Apart from the Renaissance suite, bedrooms are ordinary but comfortable

FOOD breakfast, lunch, dinner **PRICE** €-€€€ **ROOMS** 32 double, all with bath or shower, phone, TV, minibar **CREDIT CARDS** AE, DC, EC, MC, V **CHILDREN** welcome **CLOSED** Jan or Feb **LANGUAGES** English

GUBBIO

TORRE DEI CALZOLARI PALACE
~ RECONSTRUCTED CASTLE ~

Via Torre dei Calzolari, Gubbio, 06020 Perugia
TEL (075) 9256327 **FAX** (075) 9256320

GREAT POTENTIAL on paper, but somewhat disappointing on inspection. Public rooms are in the original castle that dates back to the 11thC but now with some unfortunate 20thC renovations. Most of the bedrooms, which are standard modern, in a more recent villa beside. Garden with *putti*, terraces and a pool, quite near a busy road.

MEALS breakfast, lunch, dinner **PRICE** €-€€ **ROOMS** 24 double, 4 single, bath or shower, phone, TV, air-conditioning **CREDIT CARDS** AE, DC, EC, MC, V **CHILDREN** welcome **CLOSED** never **LANGUAGES** English, French,

PERUGIA

ISOLA MAGGIORE

HOTEL DA SAURO
~ ISLAND HOTEL ~

Via Guglielmi 1, Isola Maggiore, 06060 Perugia
TEL (075) 826168 **FAX** (075) 825130

A short boat trip from Tuoro or Passignano takes you to Isola Maggiore and a renowned restaurant that also offers the island's only hotel accommodation. The bedrooms are small, pine-furnished and somewhat characterless, but the Scarpocchi family's hospitality, the fish menu and the lake views more than compensate.

FOOD breakfast, lunch, dinner **PRICE** Rooms ⓔ **ROOMS** 10 doubles with shower, 2 apartments; all centrally heated **CREDIT CARDS** DC, V **CHILDREN** accepted
CLOSED 3 weeks in Nov and mid-Jan to mid-Feb **LANGUAGES** French, Spanish

NOCERA UMBRA

LA VALLE
~ FARM GUEST-HOUSE ~

Loc. Colle, Nocera Umbra, 06020 Perugia
TEL (0742) 810329 **FAX** (0742) 810666

O FF THE MAIN Perugia-Assisi drag but still accessible, visitors will enjoy the peaceful hilltop location of this 18thC stone farmhouse, the dining-room with its long wooden tables and wine-barrels and the reasonable prices. Accommo-dation is simple but adequate and the surrounding countryside makes for some lovely drives

FOOD breakfast, lunch, dinner **PRICE** ⓔ **ROOMS** 4 double, two bathrooms shared
CREDIT CARDS AE **CHILDREN** welcome **CLOSED** never **LANGUAGES** some English

PACIANO

LOCANDA DELLA ROCCA
~ VILLAGE HOTEL ~

Viale Roma 4, Paciano, 06060 Perugia
TEL (075) 830236 **FAX** (075) 830155

I N THE REMARKABLY PRESERVED medieval village of Paciano, Luigi Buitoni and his wife, Caterina, have turned an old olive press into an attractive restaurant (cooking courses available), and given over seven bedrooms in their palazzo to guests. Their style and taste makes the most of the buildings' characteristic features without stinting on comfort

FOOD breakfast, lunch, dinner **PRICES** ⓔⓔ **ROOMS** 7 double, all with bath or shower **CREDIT CARDS** AE, DC, EC, MC, V **CHILDREN** welcome **CLOSED** Jan to Feb; restaurant, never **LANGUAGES** English

PERUGIA

BRUFANI
~ Town hotel ~

Piazza Italia 12, 06100 Perugia
Tel (075) 5732541 **Fax** (075) 5720210

IMPOSING FOYER with plush couches and copies of classical statues set in wall niches. Unusually for a town hotel, some of the bedrooms have views of the Umbrian countryside, stretching to Assisi and Todi on the horizon. Refined atmosphere and high prices attract an up-market clientèle.

Food breakfast, lunch, dinner **Price** ©©©-©©©© **Rooms** 3 single, 16 double, 5 suites, all with bath or shower, phone, TV, minibar, air-conditioning, safe **Credit cards** AE, DC, EC, V **Children** welcome **Closed** never **Languages** English

LOCANDA DELLA POSTA
~ Town hotel ~

Corso Vanucci 97, 06100 Perugia
Tel (075) 5728925 **Fax** (075) 5722413

PRIME LOCATION on Perugia's renowned Corso Vanucci where the Perugini religiously take their evening *passegiata*. Famous as a hotel for more than two hundred years, its previous guests included Goethe, Hans-Christian Andersen and Frederick III of Prussia. Rooms are stylish.

Food breakfast **Price** ©©-©©© **Rooms** 12 single, 26 double, 1 suite, all with bath or shower, phone, TV, minibar, central heating, air-conditioning **Credit cards** AE, DC, EC, MC, V **Children** welcome **Closed** never **Languages** English, French English

LA CERQUA
~ Farm guest-house ~

Loc. San Salvatore, Pietralunga, 06026 Perugia
Tel (075) 9460283 **Fax** (075) 9462033

AN EXCELLENT BARGAIN for those who like the quiet rural life. Situated in panoramic northern Umbria between Citta di Castello and Gubbio and decorated in authentic rustic style, guests of La Cerqua can enjoy long walks in the oak forests between meals of hearty Umbrian fare. Small lake for fishing nearby.

Food breakfast, lunch, dinner **Price** © **Rooms** 5 double, 2 suites, all with bath or shower **Credit cards** AE, EC, MC, V **Children** welcome **Closed** Jan **Languages** English, French

PERUGIA

SCRITTO DI GUBBIO

CASTELLO DI PETROIA
~ CASTLE ~

Loc. Petroia, Scritto di Gubbio, 06024 Perugia
TEL (075) 920109, 920287 **FAX** (075) 920108

THIS IS ABOUT as authentic as you can get: a 13thC castle hardly touched by time (except for the addition of essential modern conveniences) offering a few rooms to travellers. Stark, romantic, isolated on its hilltop, it will appeal to walkers and those in retreat from modern life. Heavy rustic furniture predominates.

FOOD breakfast, dinner on request **PRICE** ©-©© **ROOMS** 4 double, 1 suite, all with bath or shower **CREDIT CARDS** not accepted **CHILDREN** welcome **CLOSED** Jan to Mar **LANGUAGES** English

SPOLETO

IL BARBAROSSA
~ COUNTRY HOTWL ~

Via Licina 12, Spoleto, 06049 Perugia
TEL (0743) 43644 **FAX** (0743) 222060

VERY REASONABLY PRICED for such swanky furnishing (black leather, antiques, marble) but this may be a new hotel's bid for customers. We preferred the interiors, which are finely done, to the exterior, which is bare and excessively lit for the extensive car park. This is no more than a useful back-up address: reports welcome

FOOD breakfast, lunch, dinner **PRICE** ©-©© **ROOMS** 1 single, 9 double, all with bath or shower, phone, TV, minibar, air-conditioning **CREDIT CARDS** AE, DC, EC, MC, V **CHILDREN** welcome **CLOSED** never **LANGUAGES** English, French

TODI

BRAMANTE
~ FORMER CONVENT ~

Via Orvietana 48, Todi, 06059 Perugia
TEL (075) 8948381/2 **FAX** (075) 8948074

A USEFUL ADDRESS just outside Todi, below Bramante's famous church. The 14thC convent has been modernised with none too light a hand, but some character remains. The restaurant is more stylish than the other public rooms and has a fine terrace with a view. Most bedrooms are standard, with a few exceptions. Swimming-pool; tennis court.

FOOD Breakfast, lunch, dinner **PRICE** ©© **ROOMS** 40 double, 1 single, two suites, all with bath or shower, phone, TV, air-conditioning, minibar **CREDIT CARDS** AE, DC, EC, MC, V **CHILDREN** welcome **CLOSED** never **LANGUAGES** English

PERUGIA/TERNI

TODI

FONTE CESIA
~ TOWN HOTEL ~

Via Lorenzo Lonj 3, Todi, 06059 Perugia
TEL (075) 8943737 **FAX** (075) 8944677

COULD HAVE BEEN a great hotel – a 17thC palace right in the heart of Todi – but we felt that modernization had been taken too far, overwhelming the original character of the building with excessive plushness and jarring contemporary decoration. But do not be too put off: it's value for money and right outside is Todi

MEALS breakfast, lunch, dinner **PRICE** ©©© **ROOMS** 32 double, 2 singles, 5 suites, all with bath or shower, phone, TV, minibar, air-conditioning **CREDIT CARDS** AE, DC, EC, MC, V **CHILDREN** welcome **CLOSED** never; restaurant only, Wed **LANGUAGES** English, French, German

VALFABBRICA

CASTELLO DI GIOMICI
~ SELF-CATERING CASTLE APARTMENTS ~

Il Castello di Giomici, 06029 Valfabbrica, 06029 Perugia
TEL (075) 901243 **FAX** (075) 901713

THE 12thC HAMLET which makes up Castello di Giomici tops a wooded hill above the peaceful valley of Valfabbrica. Much of it has now been converted by Luciano Vagni into self-catering apartments, each furnished with smart rustic simplicity. Garden, swimming-pool. No nearby restaurants.

FOOD none **PRICE** apartments ©, minimum3 nights Rooms 4 apartments, for up to 8 Facilities each apartment has bedroom, bathroom, sitting-room, cooking facilities **CREDIT CARDS** none **CHILDREN** accepted **CLOSED** never **LANGUAGES** English, German, Dutch

FICULLE (TERNI)

LA CASELLA
~ RESTORED HAMLET ~

Loc. Ficulle, 05016 Terni
TEL (0763) 86075 **FAX** (0763) 86684

LA CASELLA, a hamlet of 12 houses built from local stone in the wooded hills north of Orvieto and isolated from the rest of the world by 7 km of unsurfaced road, is definitely for those in search of peace and quiet. A convivial atmosphere. Communal dining, attractive bar plus swimming-pool and tennis.

FOOD breakfast, lunch, dinner **PRICE** ©-©© (DB&B) ©©© (full board) **ROOMS** 15 double, all with bath or shower **CREDIT CARDS** AE, DC, EC, MC, V **CHILDREN** welcome **CLOSED** never **LANGUAGES** English, French, Spanish, Danish

TERNI

FONTE GAIA
~ COUNTRY HOTEL ~

Loc. Racognano, 05030 Montefranco, 05030 Terni
TEL (0744) 388621 **FAX** (0744) 388598

USEFUL OVERNIGHT ACCOMMODATION for those travelling towards the Central Appennines. Pretty enough on the outside, although the fading Sixties interior is in need of a refit. A change of management is anticipated – reports welcome.

FOOD breakfast, lunch, dinner **PRICE** rooms € with breakfast **ROOMS** 16 double, 2 single, 2 suites, all with bath or shower, television, minibar, central-heating **CREDIT CARDS** AE, DC, MC, V **CLOSED** never **LANGUAGES** English, French, German

INDEX OF HOTEL NAMES

In this index, hotels are arranged in order of the first distinctive part of their names. Very common prefixes such as 'Hotel', 'Albergo', 'Il', 'La', 'Dei' and 'Delle' are omitted. More descriptive words such as 'Casa', 'Castello', 'Locanda' and 'Villa' are included.

INDEX OF HOTEL NAMES

INDEX OF HOTEL NAMES

INDEX OF HOTEL NAMES

INDEX OF HOTEL NAMES

INDEX OF HOTEL NAMES

INDEX OF HOTEL NAMES

INDEX OF HOTEL LOCATIONS

In this index, hotels are arranged in order of the names of the cities, towns or villages they are in or near. Hotels located in a very small village may be indexed under a larger place nearby. An index by hotel name precedes this one.

A

B

C and D

INDEX OF HOTEL LOCATIONS

F

INDEX OF HOTEL LOCATIONS

INDEX OF HOTEL LOCATIONS

INDEX OF HOTEL LOCATIONS

INDEX OF HOTEL LOCATIONS

SPECIAL OFFERS

Buy your *Charming Small Hotel Guide* by post directly
from the publisher and you'll get a worthwhile discount. *

Titles available:	Retail price	Discount price
Austria	£10.99	£9.50
Britain	£11.99	£10.50
France	£11.99	£10.50
France: Bed & Breakfast	£10.99	£9.50
Germany	£9.99	£8.50
Greece	£10.99	£9.50
Ireland	£9.99	£8.50
Italy	£11.99	£10.50
Paris	£10.99	£9.50
Southern France	£10.99	£9.50
Spain	£10.99	£9.50
Switzerland	£9.99	£8.50
USA: New England	£10.99	£9.50
Venice and North-East Italy	£10.99	£9.50

Please send your order to:

Book Sales,

Duncan Petersen Publishing Ltd,

31 Ceylon Road, London W14 OPY

enclosing: 1) the title you require and number of copies

2) your name and address

3) your cheque made out to:

Duncan Petersen Publishing Ltd

*Offer applies to this edition and to UK only.

Visit charmingsmallhotels.co.uk
Our website has expanded enormously since its launch and continues to grow. It's the best research tool on the web for our kind of hotel.

Exchange rates
As we went to press, $1 bought 1.02 euros and £1 bought 1.58 euros